The Future of Private

The Future of Private Pension Plans

Norman B. Ture

With Barbara A. Fields

American Enterprise Institute for Public Policy Research
Washington, D.C.

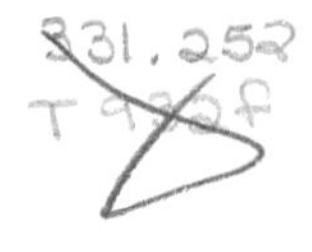

Norman B. Ture is president of Norman B. Ture, Inc., an economic consulting firm in Washington, D.C.

Barbara A. Fields is an economist with Norman B. Ture, Inc.

Printed in the United States of America

Library of Congress Cataloging in Publication Data

Ture, Norman B
The future of private pension plans.

(Social security and retirement policy ; 1) (AEI studies ; 133)
1. Pension trust—United States. I. Fields, Barbara, 1945– joint author. II. Title. III. Series.
IV. Series: American Enterprise Institute for Public Policy Research. AEI studies ; 133.
HD7106.U5T87 331.2′52′0973 76-54686
ISBN 0-8447-3231-1

CONTENTS

LIST OF TABLES

SUMMARY

The Expanding Role of the Private Pension System

The growth of public and private institutions for providing retirement income is one of the most dramatic economic phenomena of twentieth-century America. At the turn of the century, all but a relative handful of the working force relied on their own saving or on charity for an income when their working days were over. Today, over 90 percent of the entire work force is covered by the social security system or state and local government retirement programs, and approximately half of the employees in private, nonfarm business establishments are participants in private pension plans. Within a span of seventy-five years, primary responsibility for supplying retirement income has shifted very substantially from the individual to public and private institutions.

Most of this growth, particularly that of the private pension system, has occurred in the relatively recent past, since the end of World War II. In 1940, 4.1 million employees—12.2 percent of private nonagricultural employment—participated in private pension plans; in 1973, the number had increased more than eightfold to 33.1 million employees, roughly 49 percent of private nonagricultural employment. In 1950 private insured and noninsured pension plans paid $370 million in retirement benefits to 450,000 annuitants; in 1973, benefits totaling $11,235 million were paid to 6,095,000 annuitants. Employer and employee contributions to private plans in 1973 were $22.1 billion, over ten times the 1950 total. As a fraction of total compensation, contributions to private plans more than doubled—from 1.6 percent to 3.4 percent—over this period.

The significance of the rapid expansion of private pension fund contributions is not fully captured by measuring their share of total employee compensation. The salient distinction is that, unlike cash (or in-kind) wages and salaries, pension fund contributions enter immediately and fully into the private sector's saving. So, too, do the undistributed earnings of the pension funds. The net saving effected through pension funds, that is, contributions and earnings less benefits, has been an increasingly important part of total personal saving and a major source of funds to the nation's capital markets. At the end of 1973, the accumulated reserves of private pension plans were $188.3 billion. Through their participation in private pension plans, workers have acquired a substantial equity in a highly diversified portfolio of corporate stocks and corporate and government bonds. In 1974, private pension plans were the source of $16.8 billion of the $176.2 billion advanced to nonfinancial sectors in the credit markets. The investments by funded state and local government pension plans bring the sum advanced by all pension plans to over 16 percent of the funds supplied in the credit markets in that year. A considerable part of private pension plan net saving represents an increase in total private saving (compared with levels that otherwise would have been attained), not merely a substitution of the plans for workers saving on their own. Not only have pension funds become major participants in the nation's financial markets, they have also contributed positively to private capital formation.

Prospective changes in the opportunities for and impediments to the growth of private pension plans are likely to affect significantly the interests of individual participants. Associated with but transcending individual interests is the future effectiveness of the private pension system in mobilizing and allocating saving to meet the nation's surging demands for capital.

In an effort to identify and to assess the importance of past influences on private pension plan growth, the study focuses initially on the development of private plans since the early 1940s (Chapters 1 and 2). From this perspective, the study examines likely changes in the nation's economic structure, demography, and public policy developments—particularly the probable course of the social security system, the 1974 pension legislation, and the prospects for increases in the general level of prices at rates significantly greater than those which have prevailed over most of the post-World War II period—and analyzes their impact on the future operations and development of the private retirement system (Chapter 3).

Factors Influencing the Growth of Private Pensions

A broad consensus has developed concerning the major factors contributing to the growth of private pension funds. These include changes in the structure of the economy and in a wide range of demographic characteristics, and various institutional developments, for example, the expanding social security system and the increasing scope of the income tax. The broadest of these changes—those in the characteristics of economic activity and in demography—are best perceived as having provided the necessary conditions for the establishment and growth of the private pension system, rather than as having impelled that growth.

Whatever the influence of demographic and economic changes, the development of the private pension system would not have been so broadly based and so rapid had the plans not afforded substantial efficiency gains—reductions in the cost of saving—to the individual participants. These efficiency gains derive from (1) the favorable tax provisions pertaining to this form of saving and (2) information, transaction, and management economies, and the greater capacity for portfolio diversification. The former are the result of structural changes in the income tax during and following World War II which had the effect of exposing to taxation a substantially larger proportion of the income of a much larger number of wage and salary workers, while sheltering their pension fund saving from the increase in tax burden. The latter efficiency gains are inherent features of institutionalized saving, in general, and are essentially functions of the far larger scale of a pension plan's activities relative to the saving and investing capacity of the average worker.

Efficiency Gains Provided by Private Pension Plans

The more obvious but not necessarily the more consequential gains provided pension plan participants are the tax benefits. If the covered employee were to receive additional wage and salary payments in lieu of his employer's pension contribution to a pension plan on his behalf, this additional taxable income would be taxed at the employee's marginal tax rate, and if he were to save this incremental wage, so too would be the annual return on this saving. In contrast, his pension fund saving—his employer's contribution to the pension fund and the fund's earnings thereupon—is excluded from his current adjusted gross and taxable income. Although his retirement benefits are taxable when received, the employee's marginal tax rate during retirement is likely to be substantially lower; moreover, this income may be subject to the retirement income tax credit. The present value of the gain from these tax savings, obviously, is highly sensitive to the individual's marginal tax rate.

The other important source of the efficiency gains afforded by private pension plans are the advantages available to saving in this form with respect to portfolio diversification and investment costs. The average worker's annual saving, even including his employer's pension contribution on his behalf, is so limited as to preclude effective diversification; the information and transaction costs per dollar of saving which he would incur in an attempt to diversify would be far greater than those of the pension plan.

Information, transaction, and management costs for individuals' discretionary saving vary substantially; hence a measure of the efficiency gains private pension plans provide in these respects is not readily obtainable. A rough measure of the overall efficiency gains associated with pension fund saving, however, may be obtained by comparing (1) the average annual contribution per covered employee over the period 1953–1972 in noninsured pension funds with (2) the amount of saving the average worker would have had to invest in a passbook savings account each year in order to achieve the same accumulation as the pension funds. This type of investment may be viewed as one which minimizes the worker's information, transaction, and management costs. Assuming a level annual pension fund contribution and savings account deposit, the average annual accumulation rate in the pension fund is about 7.09 percent compared with 1.0 percent on the worker's fully taxed saving in a savings account. The combined efficiency gains from the favorable tax treatment and portfolio diversification is approximately 85.9 percent as of the end of the period.

Effects of Social Security on Private Saving and Pension Plans

The influence of social security on the growth of private plans has been variously viewed. The conclusions of some research imply that social security tends to augment, not decrease, the total private saving of covered workers by increasing their awareness of and concern about retirement income prospects. The severity of the earnings test imposed on continuing employment after benefit-eligibility age is also seen as having impelled more nearly complete retirement of covered workers at an earlier age, increasing the period over which retirement income must be spread and, therefore, increasing their saving for retirement.

On the other hand, various arguments are advanced that the growth of the social security system must have inhibited total private saving, including pension fund saving. The simplistic view is that payroll taxes, by reducing workers' current disposable income, necessarily reduce their saving, the extent of the reduction depending on their marginal propensity to save. A more sophisticated analysis holds that by increasing workers' real wealth, social security increases their consumption out of current disposable income, hence reduces their current saving. This is a variant of the view that the amount workers save is geared to the attainment of a targeted amount of future income, deemed to be a fixed proportion of current or permanent income, and that the introduction of social security benefits and any subsequent increase in such benefits must reduce the amount of private saving individuals will undertake to reach their retirement income goal.

These analyses do not adequately explain the effects of social security on private saving because they exclude any consideration of the functional relationship between saving and its relative cost and the effects of social security in this respect. This study presents an alternative analysis of the effects of social security on private saving which takes into account not only the changes in permanent income but also the effects on the relative costs of alternative forms of saving and consumption. Our conclusions regarding the effects of social security on total private saving and, in particular, on private retirement saving, differ in many important respects from past findings:

(1) The introduction and rapid growth of the social security system must reduce total private saving and retard the growth of private pension plans.

(2) The amount of the reduction in private saving depends on the "price" workers are required to pay for social security annuities compared with the price they must pay to purchase the same amount of future income privately; the extent of the negative impact on private saving is found to vary inversely with the price differential.

(3) Expansion of the social security system may well have encouraged workers to increase their pension fund saving relative to other private saving, if it is correctly assumed that the elasticity of supply of retirement income claims provided by private pension funds is substantially less than that of claims provided by other private sources.

(4) Calculations of the present value of social security benefits and payroll taxes of young covered workers, based on the statutory benefit and tax rate schedules over the period 1940 to date, show that their net social security wealth was negative over most of the period, implying that the price they were required to pay for future social security benefits was higher than the price of private sources of future income; the magnitude of the displacement of private saving, however, has been less than the total amount of payroll taxes.

Looking Ahead

Prospective demographic and economic developments portend a less congenial environment for the private pension system than in the past. Growth, however, will not be significantly impeded if the system continues to provide efficiency gains for saving by its participants. The principal challenges the system will face in this regard will be presented by the expansion of social security, the 1974 pension reform legislation, and the prospect of strong and erratic inflation.

Demographic Factors. In prospect for the last quarter of this century is a rate of increase in the total U.S. population materially slower than the 1.4 percent average annual rate of increase between 1948 and 1974. More important, however, as an indication of the limits on the potential growth of private retirement plans over this period, are changes in the age distribution of the population: the age group twenty through sixty-five is projected to increase at an average annual rate of 1.1 percent—approximately the same rate of growth as for the years 1948 through 1974. The population aged sixty-five and over will increase, in contrast, at half the average annual rate of 2.5 percent between 1948 and 1974.

Beyond the year 2000, more drastic changes are projected to occur. While the working age population will increase at a rate of only 0.4 percent between 2000 and 2025, the sixty-five and over age group will grow at a rate of 1.85 percent. The ratio of persons sixty-five and over to those in the twenty to sixty-four age group will have increased by 50 percent, to 28.6 percent, in 2025. These projections suggest a negative impact on aggregate saving rates. Given the projected increase in social security benefits and the substantial increase these will entail in the financing burden (in real terms) on active workers, the displacement of private saving is likely to be intensified.

Included in the Census Bureau's demographic projections are very modest increases in life expectancies. Changes so slight will be of little consequence in workers' saving-consumption choices. Substantial reductions in average retirement ages, however, would have an important impact on workers' retirement saving plans.

On the basis of census projections and assuming the labor force participation rate continues to increase at its 1948–1974 rate, the civilian labor force will increase by 32,038,000 in the period 1975–2000. The sectoral allocation of this increase in the labor force will significantly qualify its implications for private pension plan growth. Bureau of Labor Statistics estimates extrapolated to the year 2000 suggest that a substantial fraction—36 percent—of the increase in employment will be added to government work forces, principally at the state and local levels. Most of the remaining employment will occur in the private service sector, normally characterized by relatively small firms and work forces. Unless there are serious impediments to the adaptation of insured plans to the demands of small firms, however, these projected structural changes need not represent a major barrier to the growth of private pension plans.

Growth of the Social Security System. Projections of the growth of the social security system over the next fifty years, given the automatic adjustment provisions of the 1973 legislation, suggest an expansion of Old Age and Survivors Insurance (OASI) benefits in relation to preretirement income of covered workers and substantial increases in payroll tax rates or in funding from general revenues to cover the resulting deficit. Private saving, according to a widely held view, would be crowded out by the increasing share of social security annuities in individuals' targeted retirement income. This "crowding out" effect depends on workers' saving propensities being in fact geared to a target replacement ratio. But the replacement ratio concept is neither analytically correct nor a reasonable characterization of actual economic behavior. In itself, the prospect of a rising replacement ratio need not be seen as an impediment to the growth of private pension plans. It will, however, deter expansion if benefit-determined private pension plans continue to be integrated with social security, with total benefits set to equal some arbitrary and artificial replacement ratio.

Whether the projected growth in social security will more severely depress the private saving rate in the future than it has in the past depends on (1) the changes in the cost of OASI benefits relative to privately supplied future income (hence changes in covered workers' permanent income) associated with the projected growth, and (2) the market adjustments in the relative costs of saving and consumption uses of current income and the magnitude of the saving response involved in this adjustment process. Despite the apparently explosive growth in projected benefits, our calculations indicate a decrease in the cost of social security claims to future income relative to their cost over most of the period 1950–1975 and relative to privately supplied claims. Growth in the social security system at projected rates therefore implies a long-term trend toward increasing displacement of private saving. It does not follow that this effect will fall as severely on private pension funds as on other private saving. If no artificial constraints such as the use of target replacement ratios are imposed on private plans, the projected expansion of the social security system need not retard their growth. Private plans can progress as long as they are allowed to afford their participants the efficiency gains with respect to saving that have explained much of their past growth.

Effects of ERISA. The recent pension reform legislation, the Employee Retirement Income Security Act of 1974 (ERISA), is potentially a more serious threat to private pension fund growth than is the prospective expansion of the social security system. Nearly every provision—vesting and funding requirements, termination insurance, rules regarding fiduciary responsibility—has the effect of increasing the cost of providing any given level of pension benefits. If workers are unwilling to trade off current wage and salary income for the legislated increases in the present value of pension benefits, employers must either reduce their work forces or terminate their plans.

Two provisions of ERISA—those which increased the permissible annual contribution to the Keogh plans of the self-employed and authorized individual retirement accounts (IRAs) for the substantial number of employees who are not covered by retirement plans—will tend to ameliorate the overall impact of the act on aggregate retirement saving.

ERISA increased the limit on deduction for contributions to Keogh plans from the lesser of $2,500 or 10 percent of earned income to $7,500 or 15 percent. While more restrictive antidiscrimination rules were also enacted, the effect of so substantial an increase in the allowable contribution and the greater flexibility it affords the self-employed tends to increase the potential efficiency gains to saving in this form, so should increase the amount of such saving over the coming decades.

Notwithstanding the many constraints imposed on their use, individual retirement accounts offer the individual a highly flexible tax-sheltered vehicle for saving for retirement. The permissible range of trust arrangements and assets allows the individual to diversify his retirement saving to whatever extent accords with his portfolio preferences. By their very nature IRAs are fully vested in the individual and completely portable.

In sum, the IRA affords the individual the opportunity for realizing virtually all of the efficiency gains provided by employers' pension plans, and indeed, has some advantages over the latter. The single exception is that if he undertakes an IRA on his own, the individual must incur information and transaction costs which are now assumed by employers and spread over the pension costs of all covered employees; if the employer provides IRAs for his employees in lieu of a pension plan, however, even this element of efficiency gain is present. The IRA provisions of ERISA must be seen as substantially reducing, if not entirely eliminating, the cost differential between a pension plan and individual saving for retirement. The IRA, by extending to individuals the scope and coverage of the traditional pension fund, represents a significant diversification of retirement income claims. By expanding the range of saving opportunities, IRAs afford a welfare gain for eligible workers.

Effects of Inflation. The effects of inflation on private saving cannot be forecast confidently unless one can specify the inflation's effects on real labor and capital incomes and on the relative costs of consumption and future income. The variety of inflationary experiences in these respects compounds the difficulty of predicting the consequences of a prolonged inflationary period on private saving. The effects of inflation on the flow of saving through the private pension system, hence its growth, are even more ambiguous. The interaction of inflation with the ERISA and social security provisions further obscures the ways in which inflation may alter the opportunities and constraints pension plans face for reducing the cost of saving for their participants.

Ignoring for the moment the potential inflation-complicated ERISA and social security effects, it does not necessarily follow that an inflation which reduces total saving will similarly affect pension plan saving. Inflation tends to expose workers' wages to increasingly high marginal income tax rates, and so tends to increase the efficiency gains attributable to the tax-sheltering of pension plan saving. This enhancement of efficiency gain should increase workers' demand for pension plans. Pension fund saving consequently would tend to increase as a share of total saving and might well increase absolutely.

Given ERISA's provisions and the likelihood of inflation, the prospects for private pension plan growth are unclear. If inflation results in a decrease in the nominal market value of pension fund assets, the funding provisions of ERISA might well induce an increase in the flow of contributions into pension funds and subsequently into the capital markets in the short run. But such expansion of pension plan saving increases employers' costs and is likely to lead in the longer term to retardation in the growth of private plans. ERISA's fiduciary responsibility provisions put pressure on fund managers to weight portfolios toward bonds and fixed-income securities, which is likely to lower overall yields. This would also tend to increase employer contributions in the short run, but to retard the growth of private plans over the longer term.

A continuing inflation akin to that of the last several years may imply a greater displacement of private saving than that suggested by using the standard assumption of a 4 percent average annual rate of increase in prices. Whether displacement would be accentuated depends significantly on whether workers experience a reduction in their permanent income. The displacement of their demands for private retirement claims is likely to be less severe if workers' nominal permanent income is reduced rather than increased. The displacement effect might be further modified—indeed it might be more than offset—if the inflation involves a reduction in their real income. Whether rapid inflation and its effects on the growth of social security would reduce or expand the demand for future income thus cannot be generalized. Still less is it possible to forecast the consequences of this interaction for the future of private pension plans.

One of the most serious potential challenges to the growth of pension plans is presented by IRAs. Private pension plans, particularly the noninsured plans, will have to discover means for extending to participating employees vesting and portability rights substantially equivalent to those provided by IRAs, without unduly increasing employers' costs. The insurance industry, having successfully met the challenge of providing pension plans for small firms with few employees, should realize a significant increase in retirement fund activity if the same efficiencies can be offered to individuals who save through IRAs.

One of the major conclusions of this study is that the growth of private retirement plans has depended principally on the efficiency gains such plans have afforded their participants in their role as savers; the future of the private pension system will depend on its success in continuing to extend these gains. ERISA tends to reduce these efficiency gains in pension plans of the present configuration, and under inflationary conditions, this tendency is accentuated. It does not follow, however, that the private pension system has exhausted its capacity for innovations to augment the efficiency gains it provides. The history of private pension plans is one of successful adaptation to changing conditions. Neither the expansion of social security, nor ERISA, nor the possibility of an extended period of strong inflation, should impair this capacity of the pension system.

1
INTRODUCTION

The growth of institutionalized retirement systems is one of the most dramatic economic phenomena of twentieth century America. At the turn of the century, all but a relative handful of the working force relied on their own saving or on private or local charity to provide an income flow when their working days were over. Today, over 90 percent of the entire work force is covered under some form of government-administered retirement program, and approximately half of all employees in private, nonfarm business establishments (including nonprofit private institutions) are participants in private pension plans. Within a span of 75 years, primary responsibility for providing retirement income has shifted very substantially from the individual to public and private institutions.

Most of the dramatic growth of institutional retirement systems has occurred in the relatively recent past. From its inception forty years ago, Old Age and Survivors Insurance covered a substantial proportion of the total work force, but in the last two and a half decades, labor force coverage has been increased to very close to 100 percent. Benefit payments to retirees or their survivors have increased at an extremely fast pace, from $961 million in 1950 to $51.6 billion in 1974 (Table 1). The growth of state and local government retirement plans has also been concentrated in the post-World War II period (Table 2). While important impetus for private retirement plans was provided during World War II, by far the greatest part of their growth, whether measured in terms of number of covered employees (Table 3), inflow of contributions (Table 4), outflow of benefits (Table 5), or amount of pension plan assets (Table 6), took place in the postwar period. Along with this growth, there has been a continuing diversification of private plans with

Table 1

OLD-AGE AND SURVIVORS INSURANCE SYSTEM: COVERED WORKERS, BENEFICIARIES, AND BENEFIT PAYMENTS, CALENDAR YEARS 1950–1974

Year	Covered Workers (in thousands)	Beneficiaries (in thousands)	Benefit Payments (millions of dollars)
1950	38,700	3,477	961
1951	49,500	4,379	1,885
1952	50,500	5,026	2,194
1953	51,100	5,981	3,006
1954	49,800	6,886	3,670
1955	55,000	7,961	4,968
1956	57,200	9,128	5,715
1957	57,400	10,979	7,347
1958	56,800	12,162	8,327
1959	58,500	13,244	9,842
1960	59,400	14,157	10,677
1961	59,700	15,468	11,862
1962	61,000	16,778	13,356
1963	61,900	17,583	14,217
1964	63,300	18,236	14,914
1965	65,600	19,128	16,737
1966	68,000	20,797	18,267
1967	68,900	21,565	19,468
1968	70,700	22,225	22,642
1969	72,700	22,827	24,209
1970	72,100	23,564	28,796
1971	72,900	24,362	33,413
1972	74,900	25,206	37,122
1973	77,300	26,309	45,741
1974	N.A.	26,942	51,618

Source: U.S. Department of Health, Education and Welfare, Social Security Administration, *Social Security Bulletin: Annual Statistical Supplement, 1974*, Tables 27, 30, and 31.

Table 2
STATE AND LOCAL GOVERNMENT EMPLOYEES PENSION PLANS, SELECTED YEARS, 1940–1972
(dollars in millions)

Year	Number of Persons Covered (thousands)	Annual Amount of Contributions	Benefits Paid in Year	Book Value of Assets at Year-End
1940	1,527	$ 267	$ 129	$ 1,629
1945	1,976	380	178	2,500
1950	2,854	905	300	5,154
1955	3,877	1,740	555	10,604
1960	5,090	2,895	1,015	19,600
1965	6,685	4,225	1,670	33,100
1966	7,112	4,705	1,870	37,100
1967	7,486	5,395	2,125	41,500
1968	7,900	6,110	2,355	46,200
1969	8,188	6,910	2,700	51,200
1970	8,471	7,895	3,120	58,000
1971	8,954	8,775	3,620	64,800
1972	9,433	9,620	4,165	72,100

Source: Institute of Life Insurance, *Life Insurance Fact Book 1974,* pages 37 and 41.

respect to their basic characteristics. Private pension plans now cover over 39 million individuals. In 1973, these plans paid out more than $11 billion in benefits to approximately 6.1 million beneficiaries. In the same year, employer and employee contributions to private pension funds totaled $22.1 billion, representing over 30 percent of the total personal saving of $72.7 billion. As vehicles for personal saving, private pension plans have attained major status.

The role of private pension plans as allocators of personal saving into private capital formation is reflected by their accumulated reserves and by the net amount of funds flowing into the capital markets from these plans. Unlike the retirement programs administered by the federal government (for example OASDI or railroad retirement), which are operated on a tax-transfer basis, most private retirement plans are funded, with accumulated reserves invested in

Table 3
PRIVATE PENSION PLAN PARTICIPATION,
1940, 1945, 1950–1973

		Participants in Private Pension Plans			
		Active Workers		Annuitants	
Year	**Employment in the Private Nonagricultural Sector** (in thousands)	Number (in thousands)	Percentage of employment	Number (in thousands)	Percentage of employment
1940	33,778	4,110	12.2	est. 150	.4
1945	38,295	6,440	16.9	est. 270	.7
1950	45,734	9,805	21.4	450	1.0
1951	46,850	10,990	23.5	540	1.2
1952	47,145	11,660	24.7	650	1.4
1953	48,277	13,240	27.4	750	1.6
1954	47,152	14,215	30.2	880	1.9
1955	48,810	15,415	31.6	980	2.0
1956	50,239	16,865	33.6	1,090	2.2
1957	50,507	18,075	35.8	1,240	2.5
1958	49,611	18,800	37.9	1,400	2.8
1959	50,982	19,870	39.0	1,590	3.1
1960	51,965	21,235	40.9	1,780	3.4
1961	51,952	22,165	42.7	1,910	3.7
1962	52,869	23,040	43.6	2,100	4.0
1963	53,850	23,770	44.1	2,280	4.2
1964	55,186	24,570	44.5	2,490	4.5
1965	56,652	25,350	44.8	2,750	4.9
1966	58,124	26,365	45.4	3,110	5.4
1967	59,129	27,565	46.6	3,415	5.8
1968	60,257	28,245	46.9	3,770	6.3
1969	62,094	29,349	47.3	4,181	6.7
1970	62,604	est. 30,154	48.2	4,726	7.6
1971	62,844	est. 30,669	48.8	5,211	8.3
1972	64,890	est. 31,775	49.0	5,460	8.4
1973	67,215	est. 33,130	49.3	est. 6,095	9.1

Sources: *Economic Report of the President and the Annual Report of the Council of Economic Advisers* (Washington, D.C.: U.S. Government Printing Office, 1975), Tables C-24 and C-29; Institute of Life Insurance, *Life Insurance Fact Book*, various annual editions and unpublished Institute of Life Insurance data (New York).

Table 4

PRIVATE PENSION PLAN CONTRIBUTIONS, 1950–1973
(dollars in billions)

Year	Compensation of Employees in the Private Nonagricultural Sector	Total Contributions to Private Pension Funds	Contributions as a Percentage of Compensation
1950	$133.9	$ 2.1	1.6
1951	153.6	2.7	1.8
1952	164.5	2.9	1.8
1953	177.7	3.5	2.0
1954	175.9	3.6	2.0
1955	190.7	3.9	2.0
1956	206.9	4.3	2.1
1957	217.4	4.8	2.2
1958	216.1	4.9	2.3
1959	235.6	5.5	2.3
1960	247.8	5.6	2.3
1961	253.1	5.8	2.3
1962	270.8	6.2	2.3
1963	284.3	6.7	2.4
1964	305.1	7.6	2.5
1965	328.9	8.7	2.6
1966	362.8	9.6	2.6
1967	386.8	10.7	2.8
1968	424.6	11.7	2.8
1969	467.7	13.4	2.9
1970	494.4	14.7	3.0
1971	525.1	17.4	3.3
1972	577.7	19.4	3.4
1973	648.6	22.1	3.4

Sources: Compensation of employees calculated from U.S. Department of Commerce, *Survey of Current Business*, various issues, National Income Accounts, Tables 1.11 and 1.13 (Total Compensation of Employees less Income Originating in General Government); total contributions to private pension funds calculated from *Life Insurance Fact Book*, various annual editions (New York).

Table 5

BENEFIT PAYMENTS TO PARTICIPANTS IN PRIVATE PENSION PLANS, 1950–1973

(millions of dollars)

Year	Noninsured Plans	Insured Plans	Total
1950	290	80	370
1951	350	100	450
1952	400	120	520
1953	480	140	620
1954	550	160	710
1955	670	180	850
1956	790	210	1,000
1957	900	240	1,140
1958	1,000	290	1,290
1959	1,200	340	1,540
1960	1,330	390	1,720
1961	1,520	450	1,970
1962	1,820	510	2,330
1963	2,020	570	2,590
1964	2,350	640	2,990
1965	2,800	720	3,520
1966	3,380	810	4,190
1967	3,880	910	4,790
1968	4,500	1,030	5,530
1969	5,290	1,159	6,449
1970	6,030	1,330	7,360
1971	7,080	1,520	8,600
1972	8,300	1,715	10,015
1973	9,310	1,925	11,235

Source: Institute of Life Insurance, *Life Insurance Fact Book*, various annual editions (New York).

a wide variety of income-producing assets. At the end of 1974, these accumulated reserves were $172.5 billion.

An increasing fraction of private pension fund portfolios is invested in corporate equities, as Table 7 shows. Through their participation in pension plans, covered employees have thus amassed a substantial equity interest in U.S. corporate business.

Table 6

MARKET VALUE OF ASSETS OF PRIVATE PENSION FUNDS, 1955–1974

(millions of dollars)

Year	Noninsured Plans	Insured Plans	Total Assets
1955	18,100	11,325	29,425
1956	20,000	12,500	32,500
1957	22,700	14,100	36,800
1958	28,200	15,600	43,800
1959	32,400	17,575	49,975
1960	37,100	18,850	55,950
1961	45,300	20,250	65,550
1962	46,700	21,625	68,325
1963	54,600	23,300	77,900
1964	63,900	25,250	89,150
1965	72,900	27,350	100,250
1966	72,800	29,450	102,250
1967	85,500	32,050	117,550
1968	96,000	34,975	130,975
1969	94,600	37,900	132,500
1970	104,700	41,175	145,875
1971	126,900	46,400	173,300
1972	154,300	52,300	206,600
1973	132,200	56,050	188,250
1974	117,700	60,775	178,475

Source: Unpublished data on the noninsured pension plans from the Securities and Exchange Commission, Washington, D.C.; data on insured plans from the Institute of Life Insurance, New York. Fixed-income assets are valued according to a formula established by government regulations of the industry.

In 1974, private pension plans supplied $16.8 billion of the $176.2 billion total funds advanced to nonfinancial sectors in the credit markets. Adding the funds invested by state and local government pension plans, the aggregate funds advanced by all pension funds accounted for over 16 percent of the total net funds supplied in the credit markets that year.[1] Pension funds, clearly, are major participants in the nation's financial markets; their effectiveness in

[1] Board of Governors of the Federal Reserve System.

Table 7

CORPORATE EQUITIES AS A PERCENTAGE OF NONINSURED PENSION FUND ASSETS

(millions of dollars)

Year	Noninsured Pension Fund Assets— Market Value	Fund Held Corporate Equities	Corporate Equities as a Percentage of Total Assets
1955	18,100	6,100	33.7
1960	37,100	16,500	44.5
1965	72,900	40,800	56.0
1970	104,700	67,100	64.1
1975 (est.)	145,000	91,410	63.0

Source: Securities and Exchange Commission, Washington, D.C.

this role surely has a significant bearing on the efficiency with which the capital markets perform their essential function.

Whether the growth of private, institutionalized retirement systems over the next twenty-five years will match that of the post-World War II period to date, however, is subject to question. The answer depends on (1) identification of the demographic, economic, and public policy developments which made possible and impelled their growth in the past, and (2) assessment of the future course and influence of such factors.

Simple extrapolation of the past growth of private retirement plans, on the casual assumption that past determinants of that growth will continue to be operative, is not warranted. Indeed, if for no other reason, recent developments in the social security system, the 1974 pension reform law, the surge of inflation in recent years and the uncertain prospects for price level stability are likely to confront private pension plans with materially different conditions from those which influenced their growth in the past.

Any changes in the opportunities for and impediments to the growth of private pension plans are likely to be significant for the interests of participants—present and prospective—in such plans. Whatever the influence of past changes in the demographic, institutional, and economic structure of the nation in providing the necessary conditions for the private retirement system's development, it cannot reasonably be surmised that private fund growth would have been so broadly based and so rapid had not these plans afforded substantial efficiency gains to the individual participant in his role as a saver. By the same token, whatever the effect of future trends in demographic, institutional, and economic conditions, insofar as deceleration of private plan growth also reflects a reduction in efficiency gains, the participants will sustain losses in their economic well-being.

Associated with but transcending the interests of individual participants is the importance of private pension funds for the rate and level of national saving and for the efficiency with which private saving is mobilized and allocated in the nation's capital markets to the myriad forms of capital accumulation. One of the conclusions of this study is that the efficiency gains for workers' saving afforded by private pension plans has resulted in an increase in total private saving (compared with the levels that otherwise would have been attained), not merely in a substitution of pension plan saving for workers' saving on their own. The development and growth of private pension plans, therefore, contributed positively to private capital formation. There is a widespread consensus that the demands for capital are likely to expand at a rapidly accelerating rate over the next decade and beyond; at the same time there is substantial doubt that the nation's total saving, under existing tax and other public policies, will expand anywhere near so rapidly.[2] The future effectiveness of the private pension system in mobilizing and allocating saving, therefore, will be of major importance in determining how effectively the economy as a whole meets its surging demands for capital.

The role of private pension funds as financial intermediaries in the nation's capital markets and their contribution to private capital formation is the principal concern of this study. As a prelude to analysis of the prospect for future growth, the study focuses on the development of private plans since the early 1940s. From this perspective, it then examines probable demographic, economic, and public policy trends and analyzes their prospective impact on the future operations and development of the private retirement system. Particular emphasis is given in this connection to the probable course of the social security system, to the 1974 pension legislation, and to the prospects for increases in the general level of prices at rates

[2] See Norman B. Ture, "Capital Formation and Capital Recovery," statement to the Select Committee on Small Businesses and Subcommittee on Financial Markets, Senate Finance Committee, Joint Hearings, September 23, 1975. For a contrary outlook, see Barry Bosworth, James Duesenberry and Andrew Carron, *Capital Needs in the Seventies* (Washington, D.C.: The Brookings Institution, 1975).

significantly greater than those which have prevailed over most of the post-World War II period.

The future growth of private pension plans will depend in significant part on whether these plans can continue to afford their covered employees the efficiency gains with respect to saving which, as this study attempts to show, explain much of the past expansion of private pension programs. Their effectiveness in reducing the cost of saving for participants is not likely to be wholly subject to their managements' control. Changes in tax statutes, as well as other public policy developments, particularly in the field of social security, may well alter the opportunities and constraints pension funds will face. A major objective of this study, accordingly, is to identify prospective factors which are likely to impact on private pension funds in this respect and to assess their influences. Timely perception of any such changes in the objective conditions affecting the efficiency of private pension plans should permit adjustments to preserve and extend efficiency advantages.

2

FACTORS IN THE GROWTH OF THE PRIVATE PENSION SYSTEM: 1940 TO THE PRESENT

Since the early 1940s, the private pension system in the United States has expanded at a dramatic rate. In 1940, slightly more than 4.1 million employees—12.2 percent of private nonagricultural employment—were participants in private pension plans; in 1973, the number had increased eightfold to more than 33.1 million employees, almost half of private nonagricultural employment (Table 3).

In the five years 1950–1954, aggregate contributions to private pension plans were $14.8 billion; for the five-year period 1969–1973, contributions totaled $87 billion, about six times as much. The magnitude of this growth is more clearly perceived by contrast with the total compensation of nongovernment employees in the respective periods—$805.6 billion—in 1950–1954, while in 1969–1973 the total was $2,713.5 billion, 3.4 times that of the earlier period. The percentage increase in employer contributions to private pension plans was almost twice that of the increase in wage and salary payments. Contributions to private pension plans clearly represent a steadily increasing proportion of total employee compensation.[3]

The significance of this rapid expansion of pension fund contributions is not fully measured in terms of their relationship to total employee compensation. The obvious distinction between this form of compensation and cash (or in-kind) wages and salaries is that pension fund contributions enter immediately and fully into the private sector's saving, as do the undistributed earnings of the pension funds. The net saving effected through pension funds, that is, contributions and earnings, less benefits, has been an increasingly

[3] These contributions include those of employees to contributory plans. In 1950, employee contributions to uninsured plans were 11.2 percent of total contributions. By 1972, the proportion had decreased to 8.6 percent. Data on employee contributions to insured plans are not available.

Table 8

PENSION FUND SAVING IN RELATION TO TOTAL PERSONAL SAVING

(dollars in billions)

Year	Pension Fund Saving	Total Personal Saving[a]	Pension Fund Saving as Percentage of Personal Saving
1950	$2.1	$10.8	19.4
1951	2.7	14.8	18.2
1952	3.0	16.0	18.8
1953	3.5	17.0	20.6
1954	3.6	15.6	23.1
1955	3.9	14.9	26.2
1956	4.5	19.7	22.8
1957	5.1	20.6	24.8
1958	5.1	21.7	23.5
1959	5.9	18.8	31.4
1960	6.0	17.1	35.1
1961	6.4	20.2	31.7
1962	6.6	20.4	32.4
1963	7.1	18.8	37.8
1964	8.2	26.1	31.4
1965	9.4	30.3	31.0
1966	9.9	33.0	30.0
1967	11.3	40.9	27.6
1968	11.4	38.1	29.9
1969	13.5	35.1	38.5
1970	11.8	50.6	23.3
1971	16.3	57.3	28.4
1972	18.4	49.4	37.2
1973	17.4	72.7	23.9

[a] Personal saving as measured in the National Income and Product Accounts, Department of Commerce.

Sources: Calculated from unpublished data, Securities and Exchange Commission, Washington, D.C. and Institute of Life Insurance, *Life Insurance Fact Book*, various annual editions (New York); U.S. Department of Commerce, *Survey of Current Business*, various issues.

important component of total personal saving. In the period 1950–1954, net saving in private pension plans accounted for about 20.1 percent of personal saving; in the years 1969–1973, the ratio had increased to 29.2 percent (Table 8).[4]

[4] In fact, the ratio of net pension fund contributions and earnings to total personal saving in the years 1970-1973 was depressed by an overall personal saving rate in this period substantially higher than the postwar average.

Assessing the future growth of the private pension system requires insights about the impetus for and constraints on its past development, for which we turn to an examination of the historical experience.

Several investigations have produced a broad consensus that the major factors contributing to the growth of private pension funds include basic changes in the structure of the economy, demographic developments, and evolving institutional forms, the last primarily since the early 1940s. The general changes in economic activity and in demography are best understood as preconditions for, rather than causes of, the establishment and growth of the private pension system. Supporting this view is the fact that while most of the basic economic and demographic shifts occurred well before or during World War II, the major growth of the private pension system occurred well afterwards. To be sure, some of these demographic and economic developments have been extended or intensified since the war; their major effect, however, should have been felt earlier.

Institutional changes, particularly those in the income tax and the development of the social security system, may also be viewed as having shaped the basic conditions permitting (or constraining) the development of private pension plans. In some respects, however, these changes created a direct impetus for their establishment and growth.

The influence of any of these factors should be assessed with regard to workers' demands for retirement income and the capacity of private pension plans to provide retirement income more efficiently than other forms of saving available to workers. Enormous changes in the demography of the United States have occurred in the past 75 years; had these had no effect on workers' preferences for current consumption versus future income, particularly income in their retirement years, it is difficult to believe that workers would have found their employers' contributions to pension plans on their behalf nearly so acceptable as substitutes for current wages as has in fact been true. Conversely, with an increase in demand for future income compared with current consumption, no matter the cause of this change, workers would scarcely have chosen private pension plans to provide that future income had it seemed to them a costlier form of saving than others to which they might turn.

Changes in the Structure of the U.S. Economy

Often identified as a powerful force for the development of institutionalized saving for retirement, including private pension plans, are the changes in the composition of economic activity and output which have occurred since the early years of this century. In particular, the rapid rate of industrialization and the increase in manufacturing output and employment are deemed to have been essential preconditions for the growth of the private pension system.[5]

Far more important, however, is the fact that these changes in composition were associated with substantial increases in the size of the typical work force of the firm in the industrial sector compared with that of the firms in those sectors, particularly agriculture and related activities, from which the shift occurred. This change in scale of the work force made it possible for a firm to avail itself of the economies provided by group insurance, even where the firm's plan was self-insured. The economies include not only lower unit costs for "writing the policies" and for administration, but also those derived from the anticipation that only a fraction of the covered employees will eventually receive retirement income payments from the plan.[6]

All other developments the same, it is difficult to believe that the private pension system could have grown to anything like its present size in the absence of this basic structural shift involving substantial increases in the size of the typical firm's work force. It is not the increasing proportion of GNP originating in goods production, processing, and distribution, per se, that was the basic precondition for private pension plan development but the fact that this change in composition of activity also involved a significant increase in firm scale.

This is not to assert that the future growth of private pension plans is significantly dependent on continuing increases in firm size. The scale economies upon which the self-insured plans of large firms depend have been increasingly made available to small firms by the insurance industry. In 1940, only 16 percent of participants in private pension plans were covered by insured plans; by 1970, this percentage had increased to 32 percent (Table 9). Particularly since the early 1960s, the growth in the number of active covered workers in insured plans has been substantially more rapid than that in noninsured plans; in 1963, for example, 22.5 percent of active covered workers were in insured plans, compared with 32.7 percent in 1970. From 1965 through 1970, insured plans added 4,384,000 active

[5] See Roger F. Murray, *Economic Aspects of Pensions* (New York: National Bureau of Economic Research, 1968), p. 5.

[6] As shown later in this study, the fact that employers' contributions are based on the actuarial assumption that a relatively large proportion of the current work force will not be eligible for retirement benefits does not disadvantage employees.

Table 9

NUMBER OF EMPLOYEES, ACTIVE AND RETIRED, COVERED BY PRIVATE PENSION PLANS, SELECTED YEARS, 1940–1970

	Covered Employees		
Year	Total (in thousands)	Insured (in thousands)	Insured as percentage of total
1940	4,260	695	16.3
1945	6,710	1,470	21.9
1950	10,255	2,755	26.9
1955	16,395	4,105	25.0
1960	23,015	5,475	23.8
1965	28,100	7,040	25.1
1970	34,880	10,980	31.5

Source: Institute of Life Insurance, *Pension Facts 1974* (New York).

workers; noninsured plans, in contrast, increased their coverage by only 2 million active workers in this period (Table 10).

The average number of workers per insured plan has always been quite small, and this average has decreased rapidly as the growth in total coverage of active workers by insured plans has accelerated. In 1950, for example, the average insured plan covered 231 active workers; by 1970, the number of active workers per plan had fallen to 34 (Table 11).

In short, much of the growth in the private pension system in recent years is attributable to the increase in insured plans for smaller and smaller firms. Continuing adaptation of insured plans to the situation and demands of small firms would imply that a continuing shift in employment from manufacturing to services, with the associated reduction in scale of firms, need not itself constrain the continuing expansion of the private pension system. The size of firm was an important consideration, initially, in permitting the oldest industrial retirement plans to realize the scale economies which were then translated into reductions in the cost of saving for their participants, hence was an important impetus for the growth of the private pension system. It does not follow that future changes in average firm scale will materially influence the rate of growth of the private pension system. The rapid growth in pension plans of small firms

Table 10

NUMBER OF ACTIVE WORKERS COVERED BY INSURED AND NONINSURED PLANS, 1950, 1955, 1960–1970

Year	Total Number of Active Covered Workers (in thousands)	Insured Plans		Noninsured Plans	
		Number of workers (in thousands)	Percentage of total	Number of workers (in thousands)	Percentage of total
1950	9,805	2,605	26.6	7,200	73.4
1955	15,415	3,815	24.7	11,600	75.3
1960	21,235	4,935	23.2	16,300	76.8
1961	22,165	5,065	22.9	17,100	77.1
1962	23,040	5,140	22.3	17,900	77.7
1963	23,770	5,370	22.6	18,400	77.4
1964	24,570	5,970	24.3	18,600	75.7
1965	25,350	6,250	24.7	19,100	75.3
1966	26,365	6,965	26.4	19,400	73.6
1967	27,565	7,765	28.2	19,800	71.8
1968	28,245	8,145	28.8	20,100	71.2
1969	29,349	9,049	30.8	20,300	69.2
1970	30,154	9,754	32.3	20,400	67.7

Source: Institute of Life Insurance, *Pension Facts 1974* (New York).

Table 11

AVERAGE NUMBER OF ACTIVE WORKERS IN INSURED PENSION PLANS, 1950–1970

Year	Number of Plans	Number of Active Workers (in thousands)	Number of Active Workers Per Plan
1950	11,270	2,605	231
1955	18,980	3,815	201
1960	32,340	4,935	153
1965	66,260	6,250	94
1970	289,510	9,754	34

Source: Institute of Life Insurance, *Pension Facts 1974* (New York).

and in self-employed individuals' retirement plans attests to the general awareness of the efficiency gains to be realized through pension plan saving. As long as the insurance industry is not impeded in its efforts to extend these gains, shifts in employment to smaller firms need not adversely affect the future growth of the private pension system.

The Great Depression

One of the weightiest economic developments giving impetus to the institutionalizing of saving, in all probability, was the financial market collapse in 1929 and the ensuing deep depression. While the breadth of pre-crash individual participation in the stock market and of individual ownership of stocks and bonds is easily exaggerated, a sufficient number of individuals of modest means either experienced or observed disastrous financial reverses in the crash to raise widespread doubts about the safety of individual efforts to manage portfolios. Whether or not post-crash financial market conditions objectively warranted it, the risks attached to a broad range of claims to future income must have seemed greatly enlarged. The perceived cost of saving in such forms, accordingly, was substantially increased. Moreover, the enormous losses of income in the depression severely limited individuals' capacity to save. Both income and substitution effects thus operated to depress personal saving. For persons at or approaching retirement, the loss of their life savings must have occasioned a grave loss of confidence in their own capacity to provide adequately for their retirement; widespread observation of this experience must have had the same effect on most workers.

Attitudes of this sort were undoubtedly conducive to acceptance of institutionalized saving arrangements. Such arrangements, particularly if provided by government, presumably were perceived as materially reducing the risk of loss of future income; much the same would have been true of private institutional arrangements, at least insofar as these were provided by large organizations. Institutional arrangements, accordingly, must have been seen as reducing the cost of future income.

The stock market crash and the Great Depression did not require the development of public and private retirement income plans. But these harsh economic experiences surely must have provided a setting in which such plans were far more acceptable than they otherwise would have been.

Demographic Developments

Correlative with the change in the composition of output and the increase in size of firm was the shift in the location of the population. In 1900 less than 40 percent of the population lived in urban areas. By 1940, the proportion had increased to 55 percent, and it is estimated that 73.5 percent of the population were urban residents in 1970.[7]

In itself, this change in the location of population would not appear to be of major consequence in impelling institutionalizing of saving for retirement.[8] More important, in all likelihood, is that urbanization of the population was associated with increased mobility of working-age family members. One of the important demographic developments of this century, accelerating since the end of World War II, has been the spatial dispersal of family members. This indicates that the family unit has tended to become a less stable structure. This tendency has been strengthened by the rising divorce rate. As a consequence, there has been a decreasing tendency for retired persons to continue to live with their children.

The impersonality of large urban communities presumably tends to reduce the availability of private charity and community assistance as support for the elderly which is thought to have characterized the small, rural population center. Elderly family members, it is widely supposed, have increasingly had to provide their own living arrangements and to depend more on their own resources, instead of living with and being supported by younger family members or being assisted by local charities. Workers' anticipations of the need to provide a relatively larger share of their retirement income, rather than relying on their families, would increase their propensity to save and their willingness to accept some of their compensation in the form of claims to pension benefits.

Such demographic changes, in short, presumably added to pressures for greater and more secure provisions for retirement income. Recognition of these changing needs would increase workers' preferences for saving for retirement as against consumption uses of their current income. Their increased demand for future income, however,

---

[7] U.S. Department of Commerce, Bureau of the Census.

[8] One can conceive of some reduction in the cost of saving associated with access to bigger and more diversified capital markets, with a greater variety and larger number of claims to future income available in large urban centers than in small rural communities. This cost reduction may have resulted in some increase in the propensity to save, but the effect would not have been unique to institutional saving arrangements, let alone to those limited to saving for retirement.

would not necessarily focus on future income claims provided by institutionalized saving arrangements. It follows that these developments did not, of themselves, dictate the emergence and rapid growth of institutionalized, in contrast with individual, arrangements for private saving for retirement. But they did provide the conditions in which an increasing proportion of employees would find formal pension plans an attractive element in their compensation.

Sometimes emphasized as a factor contributing to an increase in workers' propensity to save is the increase in longevity along with the reduction in average retirement age, increasing the expected duration of their retirement.[9] "If individuals have to save over a shorter working life for a longer retirement period, then aggregate saving will increase."[10] The data cited in support of this view appear, upon casual examination, to be persuasive: in 1900, the average twenty-year-old male could expect to live an additional 42.2 years; in 1973, the average twenty-year-old male's remaining life expectancy was 49.9 years. For females the increase was from 43.8 to 57.1 years. In 1900, close to 70 percent of men aged sixty-five or over were in the labor force, while in 1970 the portion had dropped to less than 30 percent.

Upon closer inspection, these data argue much less forcefully as to the effect on workers' propensities to save for retirement. Between 1930 and 1940, the average twenty-year-old male's remaining life expectancy increased from 46.0 to 47.8 years and by 1950, remaining life expectancy had increased to 49.5 years. But almost no change occurred in the ensuing twenty years: in 1970, the remaining expected life was 49.6 years. In other words, over the entire period in which public and private retirement plans grew so dramatically, very little change occurred in the life expectancy of young male workers. If, over this period, these workers anticipated increasingly long periods of retirement, it was not because they expected increasingly long lives. For a young male worker expecting to retire

[9] See for example, Murray, *Economic Aspects of Pensions*, p. 5; Alicia H. Munnell, "The Impact of Social Security on Personal Savings," *National Tax Journal*, vol. 27, no. 4 (December 1974), p. 556. Munnell appears to have measured the increase in life expectancy from birth, which increased over 31.2 percent between 1920 and 1971, from 54.1 years to 71.0 years. More pertinent are individuals' life expectancies at the age they enter the labor force and thereafter; for older age groups, increases in life expectancy did not approach this magnitude. The reduction in average retirement age is attributed to the reduction in social security benefits paid to retirees whose earnings exceed stipulated amounts and to the increasing business practice of mandatory retirement at or about age sixty-five.

[10] Munnell, "The Impact of Social Security on Personal Savings," p. 555.

at age sixty-five, the life expectancy data show that he would plan for 2.8 years of retirement income in 1940, 4.5 years in 1950 and 4.6 years in 1970. Ignoring anticipations regarding inflation and assuming a constant 3 percent rate of return on his saving, in 1940 he needed to save $28.90 per year during his forty-five working years for each $1,000 of annual retirement income he desired. In 1950, the twenty-year old needed to save $44.22 per year, and only a very slightly larger amount was required in 1970. The increase in longevity, in other words, increased required saving by $15.32 per year for each $1,000 of desired retirement income. If the young male worker aspired to an annual retirement income of, say, $6,000, his increase in life expectancy over the period from 1940 to 1970 added $92 a year to his required annual saving up to retirement. To be sure, this illustrative calculation understates the pressure increasing longevity exerted for increased retirement saving, since it ignores the expansion of survivorship benefits deriving from the much more substantial increase in the life expectancy of women.

Very much the same conclusions apply regarding the trend toward earlier retirement. Suppose, for example, that the twenty-year-old male worker in 1940 had expected to remain employed for all of his remaining life, whereas his counterpart in 1970 expected to retire at age sixty-five. Combined with the increase in life expectancy, the earlier retirement called for provision for 4.6 years of retirement income, for which about $43 (at 5 percent interest) for each working year was needed for each $1,000 of desired annual retirement income.[11]

The increase in expected duration of retirement period has probably exerted somewhat more pressure for increased retirement saving by female labor force participants. The increase in life expectancy of twenty-year-old females was larger and far more persistent than that experienced by young male workers, from 48.5 years in 1930 to 51.4 in 1940, 54.6 in 1950, and 56.7 in 1970. Between 1940 and 1970, the increase in young female workers' life expectancy, 5.3 years, was nearly twice that of their male counterparts. Moreover, female participation in the labor force increased substantially over the post-World War II period, from 31.0 percent in 1947 to about 43.0 percent in 1970. Recent data suggest that there has been no tendency for this trend to diminish. Since the normal retirement age is generally lower for women than for men—females are eligible

[11] For older workers, the effect of earlier retirement and longer life expectancy is more than proportionately greater than this illustration suggests, assuming that they have no accumulated savings.

for social security benefits without reduction for early retirement at age sixty-two and many private pension plans also permit retirement at age sixty or sixty-two—female workers anticipate considerably longer retirement periods. At least in the case of primary wage-earners, these data suggest that increasing longevity and earlier retirement would have affected the saving propensities of female workers to a much larger degree.

The effect of increased longevity and earlier retirement on workers' saving-consumption choices was probably less than might be suggested by casual examination of the data. Combining these effects with the other demographic and economic changes discussed above, however, suggests a tendency for workers to be more disposed to save for their retirement and to be more receptive to institutional arrangements for such saving.

Institutional Changes Affecting the Growth of Private Pension Plans

World War II Wage Stabilization. Among the institutional developments bearing on the growth of the private pension system was the constraint imposed on wages and salaries by World War II stabilization policies. In the face of the soaring demands for labor services, reducing the number of unemployed to 670,000 and the unemployment rate to 1.2 percent in 1944, employers turned to nonwage compensation to attract and retain not only executive and management personnel but payroll employees as well.

The dramatic change in economic conditions and the very large increases in total wage and salary income (about 250 percent from 1939 to 1945) greatly enlarged workers' capacity to save. Wartime rationing enhanced this income effect. Workers, it may be supposed, were more inclined to accept some part of their compensation in the form of their employers' contributions to pension plans than they would have been if their incomes had grown more slowly and if their consumption uses of their increasing incomes had not been constrained by rationing. While the increase in the number of employees covered by private pension plans was far greater after than during World War II, the need to find alternative forms of compensation under wartime restrictions on cash wages and salaries provided an important impetus for establishing private pension plans, which carried over into the postwar years.

World War II Income Tax Changes. Basic structural changes in the income tax added momentum to the increasing use of deferred compensation plans. By substantially reducing the personal exemption, the individual income tax was transformed from a narrowly based impost on the incomes of relatively affluent individuals into a mass-coverage levy. In addition, tax rates escalated rapidly. Together these changes resulted in the exposure to income tax of a substantially larger proportion of the income of a much larger number of wage and salary workers. With the high and steeply graduated tax rates in effect beginning in 1943, the incentive to find devices for sheltering income from tax became very widespread. The attractiveness of any given shelter arrangement was enhanced by the increase in tax rates and in the amount of income exposed to tax. The exclusion of employers' contributions to pension plans from the currently taxable income of employees thus had the effect of materially reducing the cost of this type of saving by workers.

Wartime Changes in Tax Provisions Pertaining to Pensions. Favorable tax provisions adopted for private pension plans further enhanced their growth and development. Employer contributions to trust funds to provide retirement benefits for employees had first been allowed as deductions for income tax purposes in the 1920s. In the prewar conditions, pension plan coverage and the benefits thereunder were attractive primarily to executive, managerial, and stockholder employees, for whom the sheltering of such saving from tax conveyed significant benefits. For most payroll employees, however, the tax shelter features were of little consequence in view of their very limited exposure to the income tax. As income tax rates shot up in the early 1940s, the attractiveness of the private pension system for upper-bracket employees increased markedly, and retirement benefits became increasingly important in the compensation packages of executive and high-salaried employees. With a vastly larger number and proportion of wage employees subject to tax, the apparent discrimination against these employees in the limited and selective coverage of employees' retirement provisions generated legislative concern. The response, in the 1942 legislation, was to stipulate quite broad benefit participation as a requirement for qualification of plans for favorable tax treatment: at least 70 percent of full-time employees with five or more years of service had to be eligible for the plan's benefits or the plan had to provide for benefits to at least 80 percent of eligible employees if at least 70 percent of all full-time employees were eligible.

The thrust of the 1942 legislation, given the conditions of the times, was to facilitate a substantial extension of pension plan participation. Although the legislation did not require coverage of all employees for favorable tax treatment of an employer's plan, it did substantially broaden the coverage required for this purpose. By specifying the conditions for qualification and the deductibility by the employer of his contributions to qualified plans, it did assure him tax treatment for these contributions at least equivalent to ordinary wage-and-salary-payment deductions. At the worst, therefore, an employer would have no preference between paying an additional dollar of compensation in the form of wages and salary or as a contribution to a pension plan. And since cash wage and salary increases were limited by the wage stabilization rules, the contribution to a pension plan was one of the few means available for increasing the compensation of payroll employees. Since employees were constrained by wage ceilings from obtaining increases in their cash wages, for their part additional compensation in the form of pension plan benefits became increasingly acceptable, particularly in view of the fact that neither the employer's contribution nor the earnings of the pension fund was deemed to be taxable income to the employee in the year in which the contribution was made or the earnings accrued.

The most significant feature of the 1942 legislation, from the point of view of extending the scope and accelerating the growth of pension plans, was the new set of nondiscrimination requirements. This change in the tax law in itself did not determine the rapid growth in private pension plans; it did provide, however, an additional impetus for expansion, given the confluence of factors described above.

The 1948 NLRB Ruling. Extending employer use and employee acceptance of pension plans was the ruling in 1948 by the National Labor Relations Board that provisions of pension plans are subject to collective bargaining. The effect of the ruling was substantially to eliminate union opposition to employer-financed pension plans; thenceforth, unions focused their wage negotiation strategies increasingly on this and other noncash compensation elements.

Korean War Wage Stabilization. Pension plan contributions were completely exempted from the constraints imposed by Korean War wage stabilization programs. This exemption was an important stimulus to workers' acceptance of a portion of their compensation in the form of employer contributions to pension plans and to the establishment of more private plans. In fact, during the decade

1950–1960 private pension plans experienced their most rapid growth.

Social Security. The influence of the development of the social security system on the growth of private pension plans has been variously viewed. On the one hand, the findings of studies by Cagan and Katona appear to imply that social security tends to augment, not decrease, total private saving by the system's covered workers. Cagan concluded that participation in a private group retirement program increased the participant's awareness of and concern about his retirement income requirements. This "recognition" effect, presumably, tends to increase his propensity to save to that end, implicitly if not consciously raising his retirement income target.[12] This effect, one might assume, would lead to increased willingness to participate in a private pension program as well as to an increase in the amount of "discretionary" private saving the covered worker would undertake. This recognition effect has been extended by other researchers to explain the impact of social security on private saving.[13]

Katona's hypothesis of a "goal gradient" response appears to corroborate Cagan's conclusions.[14] According to this hypothesis, the closer one approaches a goal, the greater one's efforts to attain it. The social security system, in this view, advances the covered worker toward a retirement income goal. While the hypothesis does not necessarily assert that social security raises the covered worker's targeted retirement income, it does not rule out this result. Thus, it is consistent with the finding that participation in the system tends to increase rather than displace private saving. And by extension, the goal gradient hypothesis is apparently consistent with the inference that the development of social security enhanced rather than impeded the growth of private pension plans.

Neither the Cagan nor the Katona hypothesis is analytically persuasive. The notion that workers participating in a program providing retirement income are more aware of and concerned about their retirement income requirements than those who are not creates, unjustifiably, an ants and grasshoppers classification of workers. Some such distinction might be entertained if a systematic relation-

---

[12] Phillip Cagan, *The Effect of Pension Plans on Aggregate Saving: Evidence from a Sample Survey* (New York: National Bureau of Economic Research, 1965).

[13] See Joseph A. Pechman, Henry Aaron and Michael K. Taussig, *Social Security: Perspectives for Reform* (Washington, D.C.: The Brookings Institution, 1968), p. 183.

[14] George Katona, *Private Pensions and Individual Saving*, Monograph No. 40 (Ann Arbor: Survey Research, 1965).

ship had been empirically demonstrated between character of employment (whether in terms of industry, occupational classification, or whatever) in which pension plan benefits are part of compensation and some identifiable attributes of the employees in such jobs. Workers as ants, it might be argued, seek out jobs offering pension plan saving or seek to obtain this form of compensation; workers as grasshoppers would avoid employment with such compensation elements. In the absence of such a demonstration, and in view of the evidence to the contrary in the rapid growth of worker participation in private pension plans over broad industrial and occupational indexes, any such classification is unacceptable. It is difficult to conceive why nonparticipant workers would be any less aware of the need for providing income for their retirement, or why they would attach a lower priority to meeting this need than a worker already participating.

The Katona hypothesis is even more difficult to accept on analytical grounds. It implies an increasing marginal utility of wealth, to wit: the greater the amount of one's stock of claims to retirement income, the more highly one values an increment thereto, at least up to some target level.

For reasons discussed below, participation in private pension plans may well increase workers' total saving.[15] No such conclusion may be drawn with respect to coverage by social security.

Even assuming that the emergence and development of social security had a positive effect on the desire to save for retirement, it does not follow that this effect enhanced the attractiveness of private pension plans. The implication, rather, is only that workers would want to save more for retirement. Whether they would prefer to do so on their own initiative or through a pension plan depends on which they perceived to be the more efficient way to save, that is, in which arrangement they need forgo the least amount of current consumption to attain a given (risk-adjusted) amount of retirement income.[16]

Another aspect of social security which purports to contribute to an increase in private saving—or at least tends to offset the displacement of private saving by the system—is the severe restriction imposed on earned income after benefit-eligibility age. The effect of

[15] See discussion below, pp. 56-58.

[16] Workers might prefer a more diversified portfolio of claims to future income than that implied in this argument. If so, and if "recognition" and "goal gradient" effects were significant, then saving both through private pension plans and in other forms might be enhanced by the growth of the social security system.

the earnings test is to reduce the individual's social security retirement annuity by the amount of the annuitant's wage or salary in excess of some designated amount.[17] The earnings test essentially constitutes a tax penalty on productive effort after age sixty-five, the amount of the tax being equal to the reduction in benefits. There can be little doubt that this provision has impelled more nearly complete retirement at an earlier age for wage earners attaining benefit-eligibility age who would otherwise have preferred to continue to work. This does not mean that workers generally have come to anticipate a significantly longer retirement period because they expect to retire earlier—at age sixty-five—than they would have in the absence of the tax penalty. That would depend on workers generally expecting to live longer than the actuarial mean.

In short, none of the hypotheses advanced makes a plausible case that workers' perceived demands for retirement income were increased by the expansion of the social security system. Even if valid, "recognition" or "goal gradient" effects would not have militated against the growth of private pension systems, but neither may they reasonably be construed as having impelled that growth.

Various arguments have been advanced to the effect that the growth of the social security system must have inhibited total private saving, presumably including that through private pension plans. At the simplest level, assuming that current consumption and saving are functions of current disposable income, since payroll taxes reduce covered workers' current disposable income, the workers' private saving necessarily must be less than otherwise, the amount of the reduction depending on their marginal propensity to save. Whether this reduction would be more or less in retirement saving through pension plans than in other saving cannot be specified.

A far more elegant analysis has been developed and empirically tested by Martin Feldstein.[18] At an abstract level, Feldstein presents an extended life-cycle model of consumption and saving behavior aimed at depicting the opposing influences social security exerts on personal saving. These are (1) the expansionary influence exerted by the increase in the retirement period resulting from the heavy incremental "tax" on the earnings of benefit recipients, which increases

[17] Since the 1972 legislation, the social security annuitant loses $0.50 per $1.00 of earnings in excess of the earnings test, which is adjusted with the change in average wages in covered employment; no reduction in benefits is entailed by earnings of annuitants who are seventy-two years of age or older.

[18] See Martin Feldstein, "Social Security, Induced Retirement, and Aggregate Capital Accumulation," *Journal of Political Economy*, vol. 82, no. 5 (September/October 1974), pp. 905-926.

the desired amount of accumulation to provide retirement income, and (2) the contractionary influence resulting from the fact that social security benefits substitute for the retirement income which otherwise would have to be provided for by personal saving while the payroll taxes, by reducing current disposable income, reduce current saving. The net effect, Feldstein argues, is ambiguous.

In his empirical examination, Feldstein substantially ignores the expansionary effect of induced longer retirement in the specification of his estimating equation. He focuses instead on specifying a consumption function including social security wealth. He finds that in 1971 social security reduced personal saving by $61 billion; of this reduction, $18 billion is attributed to the effect of social security taxes in reducing disposable income and $43 billion is attributed to the increase in consumption calculated by applying an estimated marginal propensity to consume (currently) gross social security wealth to the estimated amount of such wealth. For the decade of the sixties, he estimates, social security reduced personal saving by 50 percent and total private saving by 38 percent. (See Appendix A for a critical review of Feldstein's methodology.)

The Feldstein analysis emerges as a more complex and sophisticated variant of a general line of argument that specifies the amount saved as geared to the attainment at some future time of a given accumulation of claims to future income. In this view, the targeted amount of future income, hence accumulation, is thought to be in some fixed proportion to current or permanent income. On this assumption, the introduction of social security retirement benefits—and the increase in the amount of these benefits relative to preretirement income—reduces the amount of private saving that must be undertaken to attain the targeted sum. The expansion of the social security system, in other words, crowds out or displaces private saving, including that by covered workers through private pension plans. Feldstein's formulation arrives at this result, without explicating a targeted amount of accumulation, by specifying a marginal propensity to consume (currently) social security wealth. An increase in social security wealth is equivalent to an increase in the amount of accumulated claims to future income and has the same type of influence on private saving as the target replacement ratio specified in the more general argument.

Excluded from such formulations is any functional relationship between saving and its relative cost. To be sure, the view that saving is inelastic with respect to its cost, that is, the amount saved does not vary with changes in the relative costs of saving and consumption, is widely held, but it is nonetheless analytically untenable.[19]

Since saving and consumption exhaust current income, an increase in the relative cost of one necessarily means a decrease in the relative cost of the other. It follows that if saving is zero-elastic with respect to its cost, consumption must also be zero-elastic. But suppose that at a given income level, the cost of consumption is increased while that of saving is reduced (for example, by the substitution of a retail sales tax for an income tax, with no change in total revenue). In this case, if saving and consumption are assumed to be completely inelastic with respect to their relative cost, total consumption outlays must increase and total saving must fall by the amount of the increase in the cost of consumption. But this reduces to an absurdity. To say that consumption increases in response to an increase in its relative cost while saving decreases in response to a decrease in its relative cost is contrary to observed economic behavior. Moreover, even if the argument in question were accepted, it would clearly deny the idea that saving was zero-elastic with respect to its cost, so the zero-elasticity assumption is internally contradictory.

Rejecting the view that saving is completely inelastic with respect to its cost leads as well to rejecting the assumption of a fixed replacement ratio as a significant determinant of workers' saving behavior. Similarly, it precludes specifying saving as a function solely of one or another income or wealth variable.

Our analysis of the effects of social security on private saving takes into account not only changes in permanent income but also the effects on the relative costs of consumption and of alternative forms of saving, both public and private. (Appendix A provides a detailed exposition of this analysis.) In this construction, given that workers are required to purchase a fixed quantity of social security annuities at payroll tax rates fixed by statute, the amount of private saving workers will want to undertake at any given level of current income depends on the relative price of social security and privately supplied sources of future income. Price, in this context, is the amount of current consumption which must be forgone per dollar of future income. The higher the net yield on a given amount of saving, the less consumption that must be forgone to attain a dollar of future income. The unit price of a retirement income stream,

[19] See Norman B. Ture, "Taxing Foreign Source Income," in *U.S. Taxation of American Business Abroad* (Washington, D.C.: American Enterprise Institute for Public Policy Research, 1975), pp. 45-46.

therefore, is the reciprocal of the net yield. The price of a social security annuity, in turn, is the reciprocal of the discount rate which equates the present value of expected benefits and payroll taxes.

Suppose that the social security annuities workers are required to buy are perfect substitutes for private annuities. This means, among other things, that the amount of such claims conforms to the workers' preferences for current and future income and that the "price" they are required to pay is the same as the prevailing market price they are paying for privately supplied annuities.[20] On these assumptions, permanent income is unchanged by social security. Hence there is no change in the total demand for retirement income on account of a change in permanent income.

However, since by assumption social security and private annuities are perfect substitutes, the amount of the latter which will be purchased at the initially prevailing market price will decrease by the amount of the "purchases" of social security annuities. But as the amount of private claims purchased decreases, the net yield on such saving will rise, hence the price of private claims will fall from the initial level. In the new equilibrium, the stock of private claims workers hold will be less than in the absence of social security. In a growth context, the amount of private saving and investment will be less than it would otherwise have been, although the fraction of disposable income saved will be greater.

Next consider the two cases where the social security annuities workers are required to purchase are not perfect substitutes for private annuities.

If the "price" of social security annuities exceeds the prevailing market price for privately supplied claims to future income, the extent to which workers will want to substitute the former for the latter will be less than in the case of perfect substitutability. The demand for private sources of retirement income, therefore, will decline less than in the former case; similarly, the decrease in the flow of private saving and investment will be less than in the former case, while the fraction of disposable income saved will be greater.

If on the other hand the "price" of social security annuities is set below the prevailing market price for private annuities, workers will wish to substitute social security annuities for private retirement income to a greater extent than in the former cases. The demand for private retirement income will fall more than in the other cases. As a result the flow of private saving and investment also decreases more.

---

[20] See Appendix A for a further explanation of the "price" of future income.

Increases in the amount of claims to future income provided by social security must reduce the amount of claims provided by all private sources, *compared with the amounts these sources would otherwise provide.*[21] The amount of the reduction in private saving is not necessarily proportional to the amount of workers' payroll taxes. It depends on the relative cost of publicly and privately supplied claims.

The expansion of social security has probably impacted differentially on private pension plan and other forms of saving. In the normal case, the amount of employees' compensation allocated to saving in a pension fund is not subject to frequent variation. On the assumption that institutional rigidities [22] are prevalent and substantial, an increase in workers' provisions for retirement through private pension plans *relative* to other private retirement income saving might be expected. The historical record appears to confirm this observation. As shown in Table 8 above, pension fund saving has increased steadily over the postwar years and accounts for an increasing proportion of total personal saving.

On this analysis, the development and rapid growth of the social security system must have reduced private saving and retarded the growth of private provisions for retirement, including private pension plans. This displacement effect does not preclude increases through time in the amount of private provisions, but it strongly suggests that the rate of any such increase was slower than it otherwise would have been.

Efficiency Gains Provided by Pension Plans

The structural economic, institutional, and demographic changes discussed above may be viewed as exerting significant influences on the acceptability to employers and workers of private pensions as ele-

[21] With increases in the state of wealth, population, labor force, employment, stock of capital, et cetera, through time, the observed amounts of saving in private pension plans and through the purchase of claims from other private sources increase, even when social security benefits are increased. But the increase in social security benefits must reduce the amount of private saving relative to the levels that would otherwise have been attained.

[22] These "rigidities" depend on the costs incurred in changing pension fund provisions. If such costs were inconsequential one might expect to find that pension funds were substantially more flexible over time, responding in a more nearly continuous way to small changes in costs of administration, portfolio yield, employee preferences, and so on. The stickiness of pension plan provisions must be taken as an indication that transaction costs to be incurred in changing these provisions are relatively high.

ments of employee compensation. They may be appropriately characterized as delineating the necessary conditions for the development and growth of the private pension system. As we have been at pains to point out, however, these factors did not, of themselves, produce the private pension system; rather, they both made possible and constrained the progress of the system. Given these necessary preconditions, the dramatic growth of private pension plans must be ascribed to the attributes which have made them cost-advantageous compared to other saving vehicles.

The efficiency gains in saving afforded workers by private pension plans [23] are of two kinds: those derived from favorable tax provisions and those derived from information, transaction, and management economies and from the greater capacity for portfolio diversification in pension plans.

Gains Derived from Favorable Tax Provisions. The more apparent gains are the tax benefits. If the covered employee were to receive additional wage or salary payments in lieu of his employer's pension plan contribution, this amount would be incremental to both his adjusted gross and taxable income, except insofar as additional deductions (for example, the standard deduction) were allowed as a result of the extra income. The additional income would be currently taxed at the employee's marginal rate. Were the employee to save this incremental wage or salary, less the tax, the return on this saving

[23] Focusing our analysis on contributions to pension plans as a form of saving is not intended to blur the fact that such contributions substitute for current wages and salaries. It might appear superficially that the employer's contributions are a poor substitute for current wage payments because of the relatively low probability that the average worker will ever receive the annuities purchased by the employer's contributions. Indeed, the persistent disparity between the number of covered workers and the number of private pension plan beneficiaries, far in excess of that accounted for by a growing labor force, has been rather widely criticized, adding force to the considerations that led to the 1974 pension reform legislation. Nonetheless, overall pension fund contributions must be very close substitutes for current wage or salary payments. Employers' contributions are based on actuarial estimates of employee attrition rates, hence on the portion of currently covered workers who will eventually receive benefits from the plan. Since the contributions are equal to the present value of the benefits to be paid, they are substantially less per covered worker than if all current workers or survivors were fully vested in the benefits provided for in the plan. But unless employees' estimates of the mean probability of receiving benefits differ systematically, persistently, and significantly from the actuarial estimate upon which the contribution rate is determined, employees' valuation of benefits, will be the same as employers' (ignoring differences in their discount rates). Then at the equilibrium level of contributions, both employees and employers must value the marginal pension contribution as equal to the marginal current wage or salary payment which would be paid as an alternative.

would also be taxable to him as it was earned. In contrast, the amount saved by the employee in the form of his employer's contribution to the pension plan is not included in his current adjusted gross or taxable income. The earnings of the pension fund are also excluded from his tax base. To be sure, pension plan benefits attributable to the employer's contributions are fully taxable to the employee when he receives them (after retirement), while only the excess—if any—of the annuity over the employee's cost per annuity benefit is taxable in the case in which the employee uses his individual accumulated savings to buy a retirement annuity. But in the general case, the employee's marginal tax rate during his retirement years is expected to be substantially lower than during his working years. His pension benefits, thus, are taxed at a lower rate than if he had received them as additional wages or salary during his employment.[24]

The effect of the difference in tax treatment of the individual's saving in a pension plan and on his own on the amount he has saved by the time of his retirement may be represented by the simple expression for the accumulation of an annuity of $\$W$ for n years at an interest rate i, assuming the contribution or deposit is made on January 1 each year. Under the pension plan, where $\$W$ is the amount of the employer's annual contribution, the amount at the end of one year will be

$$\$W(1 + i), \text{ and}$$

after n years, the accumulation will be

$$S\overline{n}/i = \frac{W[(1 + i)^{n+1} - 1]}{i}$$

If, instead of the pension contribution, the individual receives an additional amount of wages or salary equal to $\$W$ per year, pays tax on this amount, and saves or invests the remainder, with the annual earnings at rate i also subject to tax, the amount at the end of one year will be

$$\$W(1 - t)(1 + i\,[1 - t]\,), \text{ and}$$

after n years, the accumulation will be

$$S'\overline{n}/i = (1 - t)\$W\left[\frac{(1 + i\,[1 - t]\,)^{n+1} - 1}{i(1 - t)}\right], \text{ where}$$

t = the individual's marginal tax rate.

[24] Since 1954, pension benefits have been subject to the retirement income credit which further reduces the tax on this income, to the extent the credit is not otherwise reduced by social security benefits or earned income.

The difference between these two accumulations is

$$S\overline{n}/i - S'\overline{n}/i = \$W \left[\frac{(1+i)^{n+1} - (1+i\,[1-t]\,)^{n+1}}{i} \right].$$

To illustrate the magnitude of this difference, assume that $i = 8$ percent, $t = 25$ percent, and $n = 19$ years. Then, per dollar of W, the individual's accumulation of his own saving amounts to \$27.59 at the end of twenty years compared with \$45.76 accumulated in the pension plan. The pension plan accumulation, in other words, is about two-thirds greater than that obtainable by the employee on his own saving. Equivalently, the effective rate of accumulation on the employee's own saving is 3.25 percent compared with the 8 percent rate in the pension fund. Measuring the costs of the accumulations as the reciprocals of these respective rates, the pension fund saving costs 59.38 percent less than the employee's own saving.[25] In this illustration, the tax benefits associated with saving through the pension fund afford an efficiency gain of 59.38 percent.

This efficiency gain, obviously, is highly sensitive to the individual's marginal tax rate. At a 20 percent marginal rate, the difference between the respective accumulations, under the other assumptions in the previous example, is about \$14.25, almost 50 percent less than when the marginal tax rate is 25 percent greater. Nonetheless, the efficiency gain, computed as above, is 42.75 percent. Clearly, the efficiency gain attributable to the differences in tax treatment remains substantial even for employees very near the bottom of the marginal rate schedule.

Gains Derived from Greater Capacity for Diversification and from Information, Transaction, and Management Economies. Perhaps less obvious but nonetheless highly important as sources of the efficiency gains afforded by private pension plans are the advantages available to saving in this form with respect to portfolio diversification and reduced investment costs. These advantages are essentially functions of the far larger scale of the pension plan's activities compared with the saving and investing capacity of the worker. Given the relatively

[25] In this construction, the cost of saving is computed as the reciprocal of the effective rate of accumulation. The efficiency gain from saving through the pension plan is computed as

$$1 - \frac{\text{accumulation rate on own saving}}{\text{accumulation rate of pension fund}} .$$

limited amount of the average worker's annual discretionary saving,[26] substantial information and transaction costs would be incurred in an effort to achieve diversification of investment, ignoring for the moment indivisibilities that would impede such efforts. Even if the average employer contribution to pension plans were instead available tax free to the employee, his annual saving would still be too limited to allow effective diversification without substantial cost. In contrast, broad diversification of the investment portfolio is feasible for virtually all private pension plans.

The more effective diversification of portfolio realized by private pension plans means that any given return may be achieved with a smaller degree of risk, or equivalently, that any given level of risk will be associated with a higher potential net return. The average worker, through his participation in his employer's pension plan, realizes the gains derived from a diversified portfolio, hence a higher net return on his saving.

The typical worker's potential return on his own saving cannot be approximated by changes in market averages. To realize the equivalent rate of return, with the same degree of risk, the worker's portfolio would have to achieve exactly the same degree of diversification as is implicit in the index itself. In other words, if the worker aspired to achieve the risk-return potential measured by the New York Stock Exchange index, his portfolio would have to consist of common shares of every corporation listed on the exchange in proportion to the companies shares' weights in the index. Moreover, each year's saving would also have to be allocated proportionately among all listed corporations' shares. Given the size of the typical worker's portfolio and the amount of his annual saving, his efforts to achieve so nearly complete diversification would be impeded by the presence of indivisibilities, that is, the difficulty of purchasing

[26] The amount of such discretionary saving per worker in 1972 is roughly estimated at about $310. The procedure used to estimate this saving is:

(1) Personal saving, as measured in the national income accounts, was reduced by total contributions to private pension plans, using Securities and Exchange Commission and Institute of Life Insurance data. The remainder was divided by disposable personal income to arrive at a "nonpension" saving rate. For 1972, this rate is 4.14 percent; (2) the average tax rate on wage and salary income was derived from U.S. Treasury Department, Internal Revenue Service, *Statistics of Income, Individual Tax Returns 1972,* and applied to wage and salary disbursements as measured in the national income accounts to find personal income tax liability on such income, hence disposable wage and salary income; (3) disposable wage and salary income was multiplied by the "nonpension" saving rate to find discretionary saving from wage and salary income; and (4) this amount was divided by the number of wage and salary workers in 1972 to find the discretionary saving per worker in that year.

fractional shares of stock, and the transaction costs incurred in such an effort would be extremely high.

These impediments become more formidable when the individual attempts to achieve diversification in the types of assets comprising his portfolio, as do pension plans; that is, if he wishes to hold corporate and government bonds, mortgages, and other assets in addition to common stock. The information, transaction, and management costs involved in purchasing a small amount of a diversity of assets, while constraining the degree of risk, would be substantially higher, and the problem of indivisibility greater, than in the case of duplicating a market average.

Diversification, of course, also imposes on pension funds the costs of portfolio management and higher costs for information and transactions. It is generally believed, however, that such costs increase far less than proportionately to increases in the size of the portfolio. At least up to some point, then, unit costs of management, information, and transactions decrease with the increase in the pension fund. Thus, even if there were no indivisibilities impeding diversification of investment by the worker on his own, he still would encounter higher costs per dollar of saving for acquiring the information and undertaking the transactions to achieve this diversification, as well as higher costs for the management of his diversified portfolio, than incurred by his pension plan.

To be sure, there are available alternative forms of institutionalized saving—for example, open-end investment companies (mutual funds) and the common trust funds managed by commercial banks—which afford the individual saver a degree of diversification of assets substantially equivalent to that realized by pension funds. These institutions, however, charge a fee, often substantial, for the intermediation service they perform. While typical fees reflect the lower unit costs for transactions, information, and management services incurred in a large portfolio, and hence capture only a fraction of the difference between the institution's and individual's costs, they exceed very significantly the operating expenses incurred by the average, noninsured pension fund. Over the period 1955 to 1973, annual operating expenses of noninsured pension plans averaged less than one-fifth of 1 percent of the market value of the funds. In contrast, the "sales fee" charged to purchasers of open-end investment company shares frequently exceeds 10 percent of the market value of the shares. Net returns on the worker's saving through a pension plan will exceed those he might obtain on his own, other things being equal. The portion of his current income required to obtain any given future accumulation through the pension plan is less than in his own saving efforts through other channels.

The lack of data pertaining to information, transaction, and management costs for individuals' discretionary saving precludes measurement of these efficiency gains afforded the employee with respect to his saving through his pension plan. But a rough measure of the efficiency gain associated with the diversification of the investment of his saving by the pension plan may be obtained by comparing (1) the average annual contribution per covered employee (for the period 1953–1972) in noninsured pension funds with (2) the amount of saving the average worker would have needed to invest in a passbook savings account in a savings and loan institution each year in order to achieve the same accumulation the pension fund did on his behalf. This type of investment may be viewed as the most accessible and widely used alternative saving instrument for typical workers, and the one which minimizes the worker's information, transaction, and management costs. The difference between the pension fund contribution and the required amount of savings account deposit reflects the difference in the average yield on a highly—compared with a very moderately—diversified portfolio, and so indicates the efficiency gain (or loss) associated with the greater diversification.[27]

[27] Savings account deposits were accumulated using the Federal Home Loan Bank Board's series on average savings and loan institutions' dividend rate. Pension fund contributions were computed using the accumulation rate of noninsured pension funds derived from Securities and Exchange Commission data on the market value of the assets of the plans. The accumulation rate in any year is computed as the ratio of (1) the market value at the end of the year to (2) the sum of the market value at the end of the previous year and the contributions to the fund in that year, minus 1. See below and page 49:

Year	Savings and Loan Dividend Rate (percent)	Accumulation Rate of Noninsured Pension Funds (percent)
1953	2.81	est. 8.94
1954	2.87	est. 8.94
1955	2.94	est. 8.94
1956	3.03	−1.00
1957	3.26	2.20
1958	3.38	14.50
1959	3.53	6.21
1960	3.86	6.40
1961	3.90	15.20
1962	4.08	−2.70
1963	4.17	11.30
1964	4.18	11.50
1965	4.25	8.80

To divorce this efficiency gain or loss from that derived from differences in tax treatment, the worker's annual saving in the passbook account and the annual interest accumulation are calculated as if free of tax.

As shown in Table 12, at the end of the twenty-year period the per-worker accumulation in the pension fund amounts to $13,662. The difference between the amount of untaxed savings account deposit required to achieve the equivalent yearly accumulation and the average pension fund contribution proves to be highly variable. As the table shows, the worker would have had to save $1,935.32 more in 1971 on his own, but he could have withdrawn $363.12, hence saved $831.10 less, in 1969. This reflects the greater variability in the pension fund net accumulation rate, which, of course, reflects the greater sensitivity to market fluctuations in a diversified portfolio than in the much less responsive passbook saving rate. It also reflects the variability in pension fund distributions and in the effectiveness of pension fund portfolio management.

Treating the pension fund accumulation as that of a level annual contribution of $332.69 (the average for twenty years), the accumulation rate is 7.09 percent. In contrast, the average annual savings account deposit of $474.10, when treated as a level payment, accumulates at a rate of 3.75 percent. The efficiency gain afforded by the pension fund, attributable to its greater diversification, is 46.7 percent.

Were it possible to estimate information, transaction, and management costs which the worker would incur in attempting to diversify his own saving, the resulting difference between the pension fund and the worker's own saving would, of course, differ from the estimate above and would, in all likelihood, be greater. On the one hand, the worker's own accumulation would tend to be somewhat larger by virtue of a higher yield on a diversified portfolio compared with the rates paid on the passbook accounts. On the other hand, his net yield

(Footnote 27, continued)

Year	Savings and Loan Dividend Rate (percent)	Accumulation Rate of Noninsured Pension Funds (percent)
1966	4.48	−5.10
1967	4.68	12.20
1968	4.71	7.60
1969	4.81	−5.69
1970	5.14	5.80
1971	5.30	16.30
1972	5.37	17.30

Table 12

PENSION FUND AND TAX FREE SAVING, 1953–1972

Year	Pension Fund Accumulation[a]	Pension Fund Contribution[b]	Savings Account Deposit[c]	Pension Fund Efficiency Gains (percent)
1953	245.11	225.00	238.41	6.0
1954	494.65	208.96	235.74	12.8
1955	769.89	212.07	253.25	19.4
1956	1,079.29	220.70	276.32	25.2
1957	1,341.75	233.58	220.10	−5.8
1958	1,797.33	227.97	396.82	74.1
1959	2,169.19	245.03	297.90	21.6
1960	2,569.12	245.10	304.45	24.2
1961	3,238.54	242.11	547.86	126.3
1962	3,394.62	250.28	23.01	−90.8
1963	4,064.33	257.07	507.01	97.2
1964	4,858.44	293.01	599.18	104.5
1965	5,643.14	328.27	554.64	69.0
1966	5,701.18	364.43	−186.42	−151.2
1967	6,840.42	395.45	833.42	110.8
1968	7,820.13	427.36	627.95	46.9
1969	7,815.69	467.98	−363.12	−177.6
1970	8,828.60	528.92	581.30	9.9
1971	11,973.40	606.83	2,542.15	318.9
1972	13,661.73	673.43	992.08	47.3

[a] Based on computed accumulation rates of noninsured private pension funds. Calculated from Securities and Exchange Commission unpublished data.

[b] Average contributions per covered worker to noninsured private pension funds calculated from Institute of Life Insurance data. Contributions and deposits are assumed to be made on the first day of the year.

[c] Based on the Federal Home Loan Bank Board's series on average savings and loan institutions' dividend rates.

would be reduced by the information, transaction, and management costs he would incur. Assuming any significant scale economies with respect to such costs, they would very likely be far larger per dollar of the worker's own saving than per dollar of saving in the fund.

Combined Efficiency Gains. Taking into account differences in tax treatment as well as the greater portfolio diversification, the efficiency gains derived from saving through the pension fund for the average covered worker may also be roughly estimated for the period 1953–1972. As in the preceding exercise, it is assumed that, in lieu of saving through his employer's pension fund, the worker would elect to save by depositing with a savings and loan institution.

For purposes of this estimate, it is assumed that the wage or salary of the average worker covered by a pension plan was the same each year as the average wage for all workers in the private, nonagricultural business sector. The worker's marginal tax rate applicable to relatively small amounts of additional income was computed on the basis of standard assumptions about the number of personal exemptions and deductions claimed by individual taxpayers in the adjusted gross income interval in which the average wage fell each year. This marginal tax rate was then applied to the average dividend rate payable on savings and loan passbook accounts each

Table 13

PENSION FUND AND FULLY TAXED SAVING, 1953–1972

Year	Pension Fund Accumulation	Pension Fund Contribution	Worker's Pretax Income Required [a]	Savings Account Deposit	Savings Account Accumulation [b]	Pension Fund Efficiency Gains (percent)
1953	245.11	225.00	307.51	239.86	245.11	36.7
1954	494.65	208.96	298.02	238.42	494.65	42.6
1955	769.89	212.07	321.95	257.56	769.89	51.8
1956	1,079.29	220.70	354.87	283.90	1,079.29	60.8
1957	1,341.75	233.58	285.11	228.33	1,341.75	22.2
1958	1,797.33	227.97	510.41	408.33	1,797.33	123.9
1959	2,169.19	245.03	390.46	312.37	2,169.19	59.4
1960	2,569.12	245.10	403.65	322.92	2,569.12	64.7
1961	3,238.54	242.11	714.29	571.43	3,238.54	195.0
1962	3,394.62	250.28	61.14	48.91	3,394.62	−75.6
1963	4,064.33	257.07	672.94	538.35	4,064.33	161.8
1964	4,858.44	293.01	796.35	637.08	4,858.44	171.8
1965	5,643.14	328.27	702.60	590.18	5,643.14	114.0
1966	5,701.18	364.43	−172.33	−148.56	5,701.18	−147.3
1967	6,840.42	395.45	1,048.31	880.58	6,840.42	165.1
1968	7,820.13	427.36	811.70	681.83	7,820.13	89.9
1969	7,815.69	467.98	−354.39	−297.81	7,815.69	175.7
1970	8,828.60	528.92	800.29	656.24	8,828.60	51.3
1971	11,973.40	606.83	3,180.93	2,640.17	11,973.40	424.2
1972	13,661.73	673.43	1,331.36	1,105.03	13,661.73	97.7

[a] Equals required annual savings account deposit plus federal income tax, based on marginal tax rate estimated from Internal Revenue Service data, assuming the worker's income equals the average annual wage in the private nonagricultural sector and that he claimed four personal exemptions and the standard deduction.

[b] Based on Federal Home Loan Bank Board's series on savings and loan institutions' average dividend rate, less federal income tax.

year to determine the individual's after-tax saving rate. Then, on the assumption that after-tax earnings on the account would be left to accumulate, the amount of additional pretax earnings the worker would need in order to accumulate the same amount as the pension fund was computed. The annual amount of required saving on these assumptions is shown in Table 13.

At the end of the twenty-year period, the worker's accumulation of his own fully taxed saving and interest is exactly equal to the pension fund accumulation, as before. But, as in the previous estimates, the difference in the amount of annual saving in the pension fund and savings account varies considerably from year to year. The variance in this case reflects the same factors as in the former case plus changes in the estimated marginal tax rate, based on changes in the average wage or salary and in the statutory tax rates.

In order to accumulate $13,662 in twenty years, the fully taxed worker would need, on average, $620.02 in annual pretax income, that is, $288.33 or 86.4 percent more than the average annual contribution made on his behalf to a pension fund. Treating the average annual amount of pretax income as a level payment, the worker has an accumulation rate on his own fully taxed saving of only about 1 percent, compared with the pension fund rate of about 7.09 percent. The pension fund, in other words, affords the average covered worker a 609 percent annual advantage, on the average, with respect to the net yield on his saving. The efficiency gain is about 85.9 percent at the end of the twenty-year period.

Even if one ignores the tax the worker would have to pay on the additional wage payment in lieu of pension fund contribution and computes the average yield on his average annual after-tax addition to his saving, the net-of-tax accumulation rate is only 3.0 percent. The pension fund rate is 136.3 percent greater. By saving through the pension fund, the worker realizes an efficiency gain of 57.7 percent.[28]

The efficiency gains provided by pension funds in each of the years 1953–1972 are shown in Table 14, both where the worker's own saving is assumed to be tax free and in the case of the actual

[28] In this and in the previous exercise, it was assumed that the worker was able to receive in additional income an amount equivalent to the required savings deposit in lieu of his employer's pension contribution. In many years, however, the savings account deposit required to realize the pension fund accumulation substantially exceeds the employer's pension fund contribution. Since in these instances it is highly unlikely that the employer would increase the worker's current compensation by the required amount, either current consumption must decline or some part of discretionary saving must be diverted for retirement income purposes.

Table 14

SUMMARY OF ANNUAL EFFICIENCY GAINS AFFORDED BY PENSION FUNDS, RELATIVE TO INDIVIDUAL SAVING, 1953–1972

Year	Pension Fund Efficiency Gain	
	Tax-free individual saving (percent)	Taxable individual saving (percent)
1953	6.0	36.7
1954	12.8	42.6
1955	19.4	51.8
1956	25.2	60.8
1957	−5.8	22.2
1958	74.1	123.9
1959	21.6	59.4
1960	24.2	64.7
1961	126.3	195.0
1962	−90.8	−75.6
1963	97.2	161.8
1964	104.5	171.8
1965	69.0	114.0
1966	−151.2	−147.3
1967	110.8	165.1
1968	46.9	89.9
1969	−177.6	−175.7
1970	9.9	51.3
1971	318.9	424.2
1972	47.3	97.7

Source: Tables 12 and 13.

tax treatment. These gains vary substantially from year to year, for the reasons indicated earlier. Interestingly, there is no apparent tendency for these efficiency gains to diminish over the period.

Effect of Pension Fund Efficiency Gains on Personal Saving

We have suggested that the economic, demographic, and institutional developments usually identified as responsible for the growth of the private pension system should instead be regarded as necessary but not sufficient conditions for that growth. In other words, these developments should be treated as making possible—and in some instances, limiting—the growth of the private pension system. Without these changes, there would be today far fewer private pension plans, fewer employees would be covered, and the plans would account for a smaller fraction of personal saving and contribute far less to the financing of capital formation. But the changes in question neither required nor propelled the development of private pensions. The efficiency gains afforded covered workers' saving by pension plan participation, we argue, have been the principal impetus for the growth of the private pension system.

Suppose that private pension plans had not afforded the efficiency gains for covered workers' saving that we have discussed above. That is, suppose that the compensation represented by employers' contributions to pension plans had been subject to the same tax treatment as equivalent current wage and salary payments and that employees were able to realize the same economies as pension plans with respect to investment information, transaction costs, and management, and were able to attain the same degree of diversification in their own saving. On such assumptions, it is highly implausible that institutional arrangements for workers' saving afforded by pension plans would have been an attractive element of workers' compensation packages. The employee would have been, at best, indifferent at the margin between a dollar of current wage or salary payment and a dollar of his employer's contribution to a retirement plan.

Neither the "recognition" effect nor the "goal gradient" hypothesis would run counter to this conclusion. These propositions, to repeat our earlier observation, could argue only that the employee's desired amount of saving for retirement would be enhanced by awareness of an institutionalized, nondiscretionary saving arrangement. Unless any such arrangement afforded cost advantages of the sort we have delineated, acceptance of these hypotheses would lead only to the conclusion that the personal saving rate would be higher than otherwise, not that saving through pension plans would have grown at the rate actually observed.

On the other hand, the fact that private pension plans do in fact afford very substantial efficiency gains for saving by covered workers provides a powerful explanation for the growth of such plans. If workers' saving behavior is at all responsive to differences in the cost of buying alternative future income streams (whether for retirement or other purposes), and if workers sooner or later perceive the efficiency gains afforded them in saving for retirement through a pension plan, then it must be concluded that the volume of such saving which workers want to undertake is a function of the efficiency gains and of the elasticity of demand for future income provided by pension funds, given the cost of alternative future income streams. In other words, given the other principal arguments in the demand for future income (level of permanent income or wealth, age, amount of publicly provided retirement benefits and their cost, anticipated period of retirement, et cetera), the amount of future income workers want to obtain from private pension plans will be greater the greater the efficiency gain afforded by the plans and the higher the cross-elasticity of demand for alternative future income streams.

As derived, the efficiency gains shown in Table 14 may be construed as measures of the price differences between saving in a private pension plan and on one's own. Since the alternative future income streams are properly regarded as close substitutes, one should assume that the elasticity of substitution is extremely high. Thus, a very small percentage reduction (increase) in the relative cost of pension fund saving, other things being equal, should result in a large percentage increase (decrease) in the amount of such saving workers wish to undertake.[29]

Any increase in this saving, of course, is alternative to current compensation, not merely to other forms of saving. At any equilibrium rate of total compensation for their labor services, workers might wish to trade off current wage payments for additional claims to pension fund benefits, either reducing their current consumption or using some of their other accumulated savings to finance the same level of consumption.[30] Rising levels of total compensation, of course, do not eliminate the trade-off between additional current wages or additional pension claims but do mitigate the need to reduce current consumption for additional pension benefits. In general, the increase in desired pension fund saving depends on the cross-elasticity of saving and consumption as well as of pension fund and other forms of saving.

For the period 1953–1972,[31] as shown in Table 14, the efficiency gains afforded by pension fund saving varied substantially from year to year, with only a modest positive trend over time. Regressing these observations on time, the mean value of the efficiency gains is 40.03 percent, and the trend rate of increase is 3.5 percent a year.[32]

[29] See George J. Stigler, *The Theory of Price*, Third Edition (New York: The Macmillan Company, 1966), pp. 24 ff.

[30] As we show below, other things being equal, workers are more likely to reduce their current consumption somewhat; that is, their total saving is likely to increase.

[31] Observations for the years 1953-1955 were based on estimates of the pension fund accumulation rate, rather than actual data.

[32] The regression equation is E (percent) $= 40.02 + 3.5t$, with a correlation coefficient of .162 and a coefficient of determination (R^2) of .01. The regression results, clearly, are not statistically significant. As one would expect, they show no significant relationship between efficiency gains and time.

To illustrate the impact of these efficiency gains, we can estimate the percentage increase in the amount of saving workers would wish to undertake through pension plans in response to a 3.5 percent reduction in the relative cost of such saving. Suppose that the elasticity were, say, 10; then a 3.5 percent reduction in the relative cost of pension fund saving would result in a 35 percent increase in the amount of such saving that workers would want to undertake. For example, if a worker's annual saving through his employer's contribution to the pension fund were $400, he would want to increase the amount of such saving per year, other things being equal, to $540.

It does not follow, of course, that the actual increase in the employer's annual contribution would be equal to the increase in such saving preferred by the worker, as estimated above. Pension plan specifics are not easily or costlessly changed with any frequency. Apart from these changeover costs, the income tax statutes and regulations impose limits on the amount of the employer's contributions in relation to his total payroll. Hence, the response of actual contributions to changes in the relative cost of pension fund and other saving is lagged and damped. In those years when pension plans afforded substantial efficiency gains, the full increase in worker's demand for such saving was probably not realized; by the same token, when the measured annual efficiency gain was negative, employer contributions did not decline, although their rate of growth may have slowed. The institutional rigidities inherent in pension plans' structure, in other words, may well constrain the growth rate of pension plan saving to a narrower range than would otherwise occur.

Nonetheless, estimates of the sort illustrated above are indicative of the pressures for expansion of private pension funds. If the estimated efficiency gains shown in Table 14 are taken to be of the right order of magnitude and if pension fund saving is taken to be an extremely close substitute for other private saving by covered workers, hence if the elasticity of substitution between pension fund and other saving is very high, then these efficiency gains must have been the decisive factor influencing the rapid growth of the private pension system.

A collateral question concerns the effect of efficiency gains and workers' response thereto on their total private saving. Our analysis shows no statistically significant tendency for pension fund saving to become less costly than other saving through time. On the other hand, except for three years, the cost of claims to future income provided by pension funds was substantially less than that of other claims throughout the postwar period. This suggests that in all but the three years, workers would have preferred more of their future income claims in the form of pension claims than in other forms, and that pension funds would have tended to account for an increasing proportion of workers' total private saving.

These conclusions, however, do not necessarily mean that workers' total private saving increased as a result of the efficiency gains provided by pension plans. In a substantially perfect market, workers would seek to increase their purchases of pension fund claims and would reduce their purchase or holdings of other claims until the net return at the margin was the same for each alternative form of saving, that is, until the marginal costs were the same. The extent of these increases and decreases would depend on the cross-elasticities among the alternative forms of saving and the elasticities of their supply. If the decrease in the relative cost of pension plan saving was the result of a decrease in absolute cost rather than an increase in the absolute cost of other forms of saving, that is, if the overall cost of saving were to fall, then the new equilibrium cost for all saving relative to consumption uses of current income would be lower. Total private saving would increase unless the cross-elasticity of consumption with respect to the cost of saving were zero.

Conversely, if the reduction in the relative cost of pension fund saving reflected a greater increase in the cost of other saving, that is, if the overall cost of saving were to rise, workers' aggregate private saving would decline, other things being equal, despite the reduction in the relative cost of pension fund saving. This situation could result from tax law changes increasing the existing bias against saving, hence enhancing the efficiency of tax-deferred pension fund saving. As before, pension fund saving would become a larger fraction of total saving.[33]

Quantitative estimation of the effect of pension fund efficiency gains on total saving far exceeds the scope of the present study. Various data indicate that the overall cost of private saving has been

---

[33] As noted earlier, nonmarket constraints on the supply of future income claims that pension funds may provide impede the usual adjustment process. However great may have been workers' response to the efficiency gains provided by pension funds, their response has been constrained by the fact that employers have been inhibited by statute and regulation from promptly increasing their pension fund contributions relative to payrolls. The increasing fraction of total labor compensation represented by pension fund contributions suggests, however, that the response, though lagged, is significant.

rising during much of the postwar period.[34] In the context of the preceding analysis, this would suggest that total private saving was reduced—or its increase was retarded—despite the efficiency gains of pension funds. However, any decrease or retardation was not as great as it would have been in the absence of private pension plans. At least in this sense, then, the efficiency gains afforded by the private pension system have resulted in greater total saving than would otherwise have occurred.

Summary

Our historical examination suggests two sets of influences on the growth of private pension plans. One consists of various demographic, institutional, and economic changes that we perceive as preconditions for, and to some extent constraints upon, the development of private retirement programs. The other is the lower cost of saving through private pension plans compared with other channels of individual private saving. Of the two, we ascribe more weight to the latter, although a substantial part of the efficiency gains for pension fund saving is attributable to certain of the institutional changes. The private pension system surely would not have grown to anything like its present dimensions had the composition of economic activity and, particularly, the scale of the firm remained the same as at the turn of the century. But neither would the private pension system have attained so large a scope had it not been for the fact that it has permitted workers to save at a significantly lower cost, in terms of forgone consumption, than they would have been able to do on their own. The fact that private pension plans have continued to grow—in number, in covered employees, and in the amount of contributions and portfolio—long past the time when the demographic, structural, and institutional changes lost much of their momentum, strongly suggests that the efficiency gains we have identified provided the principal impetus for the growth of the system.

[34] This is to say that the trend of rising yields on passbook savings accounts, for instance, does not adequately measure the change in the cost of personal saving. The observed passbook rate in any year is the market's short-run equilibrium rate. If the aggregate amount of saving at any given yield were to decline—at least relative to the growth in permanent income—the market rate would rise. This leftward shift in the supply schedule of saving would reflect various factors that had increased the cost of saving. For any one individual, the increase in the passbook rate reduces the cost to him of any given amount of saving, relative to what that cost otherwise would be.

3
LOOKING AHEAD

The future growth of the private pension system is likely to depend less on prospective demographic and economic changes than on institutional developments affecting the ability of the pension plans to provide workers with efficiency gains for their saving. If the long-term growth in private pension plans were highly sensitive to changes in demography and the structure of the economy, the prospects for expansion, beyond the year 2000, would be dim. For the last quarter of this century, however, probable changes do not appear to be significantly adverse. Presently projected demographic changes point to a diminishing rate of increase not only in the total population but in the civilian labor force, hence employment, as well. Continuation of recent trends in the sectoral composition of economic output will see a decreasing proportion of the labor force in manufacturing and other large-scale private business and an accelerating shift to services and government.

More important to the future growth of private pension plans are potential developments in the social security system and prospective changes in the laws and regulations governing private pensions. The prospect of more prolonged and erratic rates of inflation than have characterized most of the postwar era poses an additional challenge. But the most serious questions derive from the interaction of these factors.

Changes in Economic Structure and Demography

Population Growth. In prospect for the last quarter of this century is a markedly slower rate of increase in the total U.S. population than was experienced during the period 1948–1974. Population growth to the year 2000 is projected by the Bureau of the Census at average annual rates ranging from a low of 0.56 percent (Series III) to a high of 1.17 percent (Series I); the generally used projection (Series II) estimates a growth rate of 0.81 percent.[35] Even the highest of these alternative rates is materially slower than the recent past rate of over 1.4 percent.

Age distribution of the projected population has more bearing than population growth on the potential demographic impact on provisions for retirement. Most of the persons who will be sixty-five years or over during the next quarter-century either are now already retired and annuitants of institutional retirement plans or are still in the labor force; of the latter, all but a handful are now covered by social security and roughly half are also covered by private retirement plans. Relatively few persons in this age group will be new entrants into the labor force, hence candidates for retirement plan coverage. The growth in this population age group, accordingly, affords some indication of the prospective increase in pension recipients, reflecting in a rough fashion the earlier growth in the number of workers covered by pension plans. Similarly, the increase in the age twenty to sixty-four population through the year 2000 affords a rough indication of the increase in the number of active workers who may be covered by retirement plans. A change in the rate of increase in this age group would therefore signal a change in the growth potential of pension plan coverage.

On the Census Series II basis, the population in the age group twenty through sixty-four is projected to increase by 37,971,000 through the year 2000, representing an average annual growth rate of 1.1 percent. This is the same rate of growth as for the years 1948 through 1974 when this age group increased by 28,641,000. In contrast, the population aged sixty-five and over is projected to increase by 8,785,000 as against 10,277,000 from 1948 through 1974. Over the next twenty-five years, this group will increase at an average annual rate of 1.3 percent, just over half as fast as the 2.5 percent annual rate in the 1948–1974 period.

While the sixty-five and over population increased in relative size, from 13.4 percent of the age twenty through sixty-four popula-

---

[35] U.S. Department of Commerce, Bureau of the Census, "Projections of the Population of the U.S.: 1975-2050," p-25, No. 601, October 1975. None of these projections reflects any significant change in estimated mortality rates; almost all of the difference among the projections derives from alternative assumptions about child bearing. Series I is based on 2.7 births per woman. Series III projects only 1.7 births, and Series II assumes 2.1 births, yielding a population replacement ratio of 1.0.

tion in 1948 to 19.0 percent in 1974, this ratio is projected to increase only slightly—to 20.1 percent—by the year 2000. This very slight change in the ratio of retirement-age persons to the working-age population, twenty through sixty-four years, suggests little demographic impact on aggregate saving rates. Even were all retirement systems essentially intergenerational transfers, such stability in the age distribution of the population would imply no significant change in the burden on labor-force participants for the next twenty-five years. Despite a stable age distribution of the population, however, the prospective changes in social security benefits are likely to increase the financing burden, in real terms, on active workers, and the displacement effect on private saving is likely to be intensified.

Beyond the turn of the century, far more drastic changes are projected on the Series II basis. From the year 2000 through 2025, total population is estimated to increase at an average annual rate of only 0.5 percent, a third of the 1948–1974 growth rate. The population in the twenty to sixty-four age group is projected to increase by 15,754,000, a rate of 0.4 percent. This is only 42 percent of the increase in this age group projected for the period from 1974 through 2000. In sharp contrast, the population in the sixty-five and over group will increase at a rate of 1.85 percent per annum, almost half again as fast as between 1974 and 2000; the number in this group will be 17,505,000 greater in 2025 than in 2000, twice the increase of the period 1974–2000. By 2025, the number of persons age sixty-five or over will be 28.6 percent of the twenty to sixty-four working-age population; the ratio will have increased by 42 percent over that in the year 2000.

Included in these demographic projections are modest changes in life expectancies. For twenty-year-old males, remaining life expectancy is projected to decline from 49.9 years in 1973 to 48.1 years in 2000. A slightly smaller decline is projected for twenty-year-old females, from 57.1 to 55.6 years. Males who were thirty-four years old in 1973 might expect to live an additional 37.2 years; thirty-four-year-old females that year had an average life expectancy of 43.6 years. In the year 2000, the thirty-four-year-old females will expect to live an additional 44.2 years.

As our earlier discussion argues, changes in life expectancies of these magnitudes are likely to be of little consequence in themselves in determining workers' demands for future income for their retirement years. Far more consequential would be possible changes in retirement practices, for example, earlier retirements than are now customary. A reduction in the retirement age from sixty-five to, say, fifty-five in the year 2000 would increase the twenty-year-old male's required annual saving during his working years from $17.05 to $104.00 for each $1,000 of retirement income he desires, assuming constant prices and a 5 percent annual return on his saving.

The prospect of reduction in the retirement age of the magnitude suggested above, which is in line with historical experience, may be qualified by recent proposals to increase the social security benefit eligibility age to sixty-eight years after the turn of the century. If this proposal, aimed at reducing the projected financing burden of the system, were to induce employers generally to increase the normal retirement age, individuals' saving-consumption patterns would surely be significantly altered. A standard retirement age of sixty-eight years would actually exceed the actuarial mean life-expectancy of twenty-year-old males in the year 2000 and would sharply reduce the expected duration of the retirement period for all workers.

Labor Force Growth. Population data and estimates, of course, suggest only the limitations on growth in the labor force, employment, and annuitants, the demographic variables that are most immediately significant for pension plan development. From 1948 through 1974, the labor force increased by 31,160,000, an average annual rate of 1.6 percent. In this period, the labor force pension participation rate (including the armed forces as a percent of the noninstitutional population sixteen years of age or over) increased from 59.4 percent to 61.8 percent. Extrapolating this trend on the basis of the Series II population projection yields a labor force participation rate of 64.3 percent in the year 2000, and a labor force of 126,151,000. Assuming armed forces of about 1,500,000, the civilian labor force is projected at 124,651,000.[36] This is an increase of 32,038,000, at an average annual rate slightly less than 1.2 percent for the period 1975–2000.[37]

Beyond the year 2000, the labor force is projected to increase by 26,947,000 to a total of 153,098,000 in the year 2025. Additional growth of 16,164,000 in the following twenty-five years projects a labor force of 169,262,000 persons in the year 2050. From an average annual rate of increase of 1.2 percent for the last quarter of this

[36] These projections are based on Bureau of Labor Statistics historical data. Our projection of the labor force based on extrapolation of the change in participation rate yields an estimate of 108,978,000 for the year 1985, compared with a BLS projection of 107,700,000 for that year. See U.S. Department of Labor, Bureau of Labor Statistics, "The Structure of the U.S. Economy in 1980 and 1985," Bulletin 1831 (1975).

[37] More rapid acceleration through the year 2000 than during the past twenty-five years in the female labor force participation rate would tend to increase the labor force and its rate of growth above these projections.

century, the labor force growth rate is projected as decreasing to 0.8 percent from 2000 to 2025 and to approximately 0.4 percent in the years from 2025 to 2050.

Projected Changes in Economic Structure. The sectoral allocation of increases in the labor force significantly qualifies the implications for private pension plans. If the Bureau of Labor Statistics projections to the year 1985 are extrapolated to the year 2000, a substantial fraction of the increase in the labor force will be added to government work forces, principally at the state and local levels. From 1970 through 1980, the BLS projects an increase of 18,303,000 jobs [38] for the entire economy of which 4,075,000 or 22.3 percent are expected to be in government. From 1980 through 1985, the projection is an additional 6,033,000 jobs, overall, of which 2,190,000 or 36.3 percent are expected to be in government. Of these, 2,120,000 are expected to be in state and local governments. If the 1980–1985 ratio is applied to our estimated increase in the civilian labor force from 1975 through 2000, about 11,633,000 of the 32,038,000 increase will represent additional government work force, most of whom will be in state and local governments.[39]

Projections of the allocation of employment beyond the year 2000 are highly speculative. One might assume that the declining rate of growth in the total population and in the school-age population in particular would slow the increase in employment in the state and local government sector. Against this conclusion is the Bureau of Labor Statistics projection of a rapid increase in such employment between 1975 and 1985 coinciding with a projected decline in the under-sixteen-year-old population. Factors other than demographic shifts are responsible for the BLS projections of a rapid buildup in the state and local government sector over the next decades. Whether such factors will lose their force in the first half of the next century so that the proportionate sectoral allocation of the labor force in those years will differ materially from the 1975–2000 period is impossible to say. Continuation in the 2000–2050 period of the trends projected to the year 2000 would result in a strikingly large proportion of the labor force being employed by state and local governments and in the private service sector.

The projected expansion of state and local government employment implies rapid growth of the pension plans of these govern-

[38] The BLS projection counts the number of jobs rather than the number of workers as "employment."

[39] Bureau of Labor Statistics, "The Structure of the U.S. Economy in 1980 and 1985."

ments, hence a substantial increase in the amount of current saving directed by these plans into the capital market. As Table 2 above shows, state and local plans have grown rapidly since the end of World War II. From 1945 through 1972, the book value of these plans' assets increased by almost $70 billion, from $2.5 billion to $72.1 billion, at an average annual rate of almost 13.3 percent. Of itself, the projected near doubling of state and local government employment from 1974 through 2000 suggests continued rapid growth of the plans, albeit at a substantially slower rate than in the past quarter of a century. Assuming the rapid liberalization of these plans will continue, their prospective growth (in contributions and asset values) may closely approximate the 1948–1974 experience.

In the private sector, BLS projections for the period 1980–1985 place an overwhelming proportion of the additional jobs in sectors other than manufacturing. Including state and local government, ten largely service industries are projected to account for 5,302,000 out of the total of 6,033,000 additional jobs between 1980 and 1985 (see Table 15). Manufacturing employment will increase from 22,923,000 to 23,499,000, or by 2.5 percent between 1980 and 1985, and very small numbers of additional jobs are projected for transportation, communication and public utilities, trade, and finance, insurance and real estate.

Table 15

PROJECTED INCREASE IN JOBS, 1980–1985

	Additional Jobs	
Industry	Number (in thousands)	Percent of total
State and local government	2,120	35.1
Miscellaneous business services	628	10.4
Retail trade	509	8.4
Hospitals	460	7.6
Health services except hospitals	367	6.1
Finance	338	5.6
Construction	276	4.6
Miscellaneous professional services	222	3.7
Nonprofit organizations	205	3.4
Wholesale trade	177	2.9
Subtotal	5,302	87.9
Total economy	6,033	100.0

Source: Department of Labor, Bureau of Labor Statistics.

Applying the BLS sectoral distribution to the projected 30,436,000 increase in employees (assuming a 5 percent unemployment rate) from 1975 through 2000, it may be seen that by far the largest number of additional jobs will be in sectors characterized by relatively small firms (Table 16). As we have seen, much of the growth in private pension plans in recent years is that of insured plans for smaller and smaller firms. Unless serious impediments emerge to the adaptation of insured plans to the demands of small firms, the structural changes suggested by the distribution of the projected growth in employment need not represent a major barrier to the growth of private pension plans.

Institutional Factors

If demographic and structural factors were major determinants of the growth of the private pension system, the preceding discussion would urge that the prospects for that growth are, on the whole, unfavorable. However, the rate of expansion of the private pension system over the next several decades is likely to be substantially independent of those factors. Far more important will be institutional

Table 16

DISTRIBUTION OF PROJECTED INCREASE (1975–2000) IN EMPLOYEES BY SECTOR

	Increase in Employees	
Sector	Number (in thousands)	Percentage
Nonagriculture	21,397	70.3
Mining	−152	−0.5
Construction	1,400	4.6
Manufacturing	2,891	9.5
Transportation, etc.	243	0.8
Trade	3,470	11.4
Finance, etc.	2,952	9.7
Other services	10,592	34.8
Agriculture	−2,009	−6.6
Total private	19,388	63.7
Government	11,048	36.3
Total	30,436	100.0

Source: Department of Labor, Bureau of Labor Statistics.

changes bearing on the efficiency gains in saving that private pension plans afford covered workers. Also important will be the future course of the general level of prices and the anticipatory market response. Although any number of institutional changes may alter the private system, two major sets of institutional factors may usefully be singled out. Prospective developments in the social security system comprise one; the other consists of possible changes in the thrust of the statutes and regulations governing private plans, initiated by the 1974 pension reform legislation.

Social Security. From 1950 through 1975, the number of persons receiving Old-Age and Survivors Insurance benefits increased from about 3.5 million to about 27.6 million, an average annual rate of about 8.6 percent. In 1950, retired workers receiving primary retirement benefits under the social security system numbered about 1.8 million, or 14.5 percent of the population sixty-five years or older. In 1975, primary beneficiaries had increased to 16.5 million, 60.0 percent of persons sixty-two years or older.

Over the same period, retirement, survivors and dependent benefits increased from about $1 billion to about $58.9 billion, at the somewhat startling average annual rate of more than 17.7 percent, more than twice as fast as the number of beneficiaries. The average annual benefits increased from about $276 in 1950 to $2,134 in 1975, or slightly more than 8.5 percent per year; this is more than half again as fast as the 5.4 percent rate of increase in disposable personal income. In 1950, old age and survivorship benefits were equal to 0.6 percent of compensation of employees. In 1975, the ratio had increased tenfold to 6.4 percent.

These growth rates, measuring experience over the past twenty-five years, understate the expansion of the system in the recent past. While the number of beneficiaries increased at an average annual rate of 3.2 percent from 1970 through 1975, benefits increased by 15.4 percent a year; benefits per recipient increased on the average 11.8 percent a year. In 1970 OASI benefits equalled 3.9 percent of total compensation of employees; in only five years the ratio increased to 6.4 percent.

Financing this rapid growth in retirement and survivorship benefits has required a huge increase in payroll taxes, from $2.7 billion in 1950 to $55.9 billion in 1975. Over the twenty-five-year period, these taxes increased at an average annual rate of close to 12.9 percent. In 1950, OASI payroll taxes equalled 1.7 percent of total employee compensation; in 1975, the ratio was 6.4 percent.

Our earlier analysis argues that this accelerating growth in the social security system must have had a seriously depressing effect on the private saving rate. Looking ahead, the adverse effects are likely to be sharply increased.

Statutory revisions in 1973 were intended to systematize changes in OASI benefits and contributions and to provide automatic adjustments in response to significant changes in the cost of living. The legislation put into effect a complex and far-reaching set of rules providing automatic cost-of-living increases in benefits to individuals in current payment status. In turn, these increases automatically increase the contribution base and the benefit schedule of prospective beneficiaries. Automatic increases in the earnings test for beneficiaries were also established.

Briefly summarized, the new rules provide a cost-of-living increase in benefits for existing beneficiaries in every year[40] when the average of the consumer price index (CPI) for the first three months exceeds by 3 percent or more that of the first three months of the year in which the last cost-of-living increase was made. In addition, each of the rates in the benefit schedule for prospective beneficiaries is increased in the same ratio as the percentage increase in benefits for current beneficiaries. In every year in which a cost-of-living benefit increase occurs, the contribution and benefit base is multiplied by the ratio of current average wages in covered employment to average wages in the first quarter of the year in which the last base increase became effective. The product, if it is greater than the existing benefit base, is rounded to the nearest multiple of $300; however, in no case is the base ever lowered. One-twelfth of the increase in the benefit base is added to the benefit schedule; for purposes of computing the prospective benefits of a covered employee, a 20 percent rate is applied to this amount.

The effect of these rules may be seen by comparison of the benefit schedules as of the beginning of 1975 and 1976 (Table 17). The 1976 benefit schedule shows an increase of 8 percent in each of the rates applied to the various amounts of average monthly earnings, reflecting the 8 percent increase in the consumer price index. It also shows the addition to the benefit schedule of $100 of average monthly earnings, to which a 20 percent rate applies; this amount is one-twelfth of the 8.2 percent increase in average wages in covered employment rounded to the nearest multiple of $300 ($15,300).

An increase of, say, 5 percent in benefits for persons in current payment status in 1977 would increase each of the percentages shown

[40] Except in a year in which the Congress enacts a general benefit increase.

Table 17
OASI BENEFIT SCHEDULE, 1975 AND 1976

	Percentage	
	1975	1976
First $110 of average monthly earnings	119.89	129.48
Next $290 of average monthly earnings	43.61	47.10
Next $150 of average monthly earnings	40.75	44.01
Next $100 of average monthly earnings	47.90	51.73
Next $100 of average monthly earnings	26.64	28.77
Next $250 of average monthly earnings	22.20	23.98
Next $175 of average monthly earnings	20.00	21.60
Next $100 of average monthly earnings		20.00

Source: U.S. Department of Health, Education, and Welfare, Social Security Administration.

in the 1976 schedule by 5 percent and would occasion a determination whether to adjust the contribution and benefit base. If average wages in covered employment also increased by 5 percent, a $75 line, to which the 20 percent rate would apply, would be added to the benefit schedule. If average wages had increased by less or more than the 5 percent increase in the consumer price index, the increment to average monthly earnings credited toward benefits would be less or more than $75.

If the consumer price index measured an increase of 3 percent or more in the cost of living while average wages in covered employment remained constant, no adjustment would be made to the contribution and benefit base, although the percentage rates applied to the existing schedule would be increased. If average wages were to increase as the result of productivity gains while prices remained constant, neither the benefits payable to current retirees nor the replacement rates in the benefit schedule would be adjusted; the contribution and benefit base would also remain the same.[41]

[41] For example, if for the four consecutive years, 1977-1980, currently employed workers realized 4 percent increases in their earnings annually while the consumer price index rose only 0.5 percent annually in 1977-1979 and 6 percent in 1980, no adjustments to benefits or the contribution and benefit base would be made until 1980. In 1980, benefits to persons in current payment status would rise by 7.5 percent, as would the percentage rates applied to various amounts of average monthly earnings on the benefit schedule. The increase in benefits would automatically occasion an increase in the contribution and benefit base; in this case, the base would rise by 12 percent (rounded to the nearest multiple of $300), to $17,700, from $15,300 in 1976. In addition, the $200 increase in average monthly earnings would be added as a new line on the benefit schedule to which a 20 percent rate would apply.

The earnings test for annuitants under seventy-two years of age is similarly adjusted. A given percentage increase in the contribution and benefit base raises by an equal percentage (rounded to the nearest multiple of $10) the amount of earnings the annuitant may have before losing benefits.

One of the principal 1973 provisions makes the prospective retirement benefits of covered employees a function of the cost-of-living increases in the benefits of current annuitants. An increase in the consumer price index of 3 percent or more, accordingly, has a compounded effect on future OASI expenditures; it not only increases the amount of benefits to those now receiving OASI payments but also boosts the future benefits of persons currently employed. These cost-of-living adjustments automatically increase the contribution base if there has been an equiproportionate increase in wages of covered employees.

The net effect of this system of adjustments on the projected flow of benefits, payroll taxes, and deficits in the OASI Trust Fund will depend on the rate of increase in the consumer price index and on basic demographic factors affecting the increases in the labor force, employment, and the beneficiary population.

From 1975 through the year 2000, the number of OASI beneficiaries is expected to increase by about a third, to 36,091,000 persons; the average annual rate of increase is about 5.5 percent.[42] While this is a slower *rate* of increase than the 8.6 percent annual average in the period 1950–1975, it is about one-quarter larger in *number* of beneficiaries. Primary OASI beneficiaries in 1975 comprised about three-fourths of the population age sixty-five or older; the ratio is projected to increase to 82.3 percent in the year 2000. The projected 8.5 million increase in the number of OASI beneficiaries is close to 30 percent of the increase in employment projected for the same period.

Beyond the year 2000, the increase in the number of beneficiaries is projected to accelerate very rapidly for twenty-five years, then to slow materially to the year 2050. Between 2000 and 2025 the total number of OASI beneficiaries, it is estimated, will increase by 53.2 percent, from 36,091,000 to 55,290,000. From 2025 to 2050 the projected increase is only 3.6 percent, to 57,306,000 beneficiaries. As Table 18 shows, these projections presage a significant increase in the ratio of OASI primary and secondary beneficiaries to the number of labor force participants. Since OASI is a tax-transfer

[42] For the projection period, estimates are as of June 30 for each year; the historical series estimates are as of December 31.

Table 18

TOTAL AND PRIMARY OASI BENEFICIARIES AS A PERCENTAGE OF THE LABOR FORCE IN SELECTED YEARS

		OASI Beneficiaries			
Year	**Labor Force**	Primary	Percentage of labor force	Total	Percentage of labor force
1975	94,793	16,500	17.4	27,600	29.1
1985	108,978	21,243	19.5	32,154	29.5
2000	126,151	25,172	20.0	36,091	28.6
2025	153,098	44,427	29.0	55,290	36.1
2050	169,262	47,020	27.8	57,306	33.4

Source: U.S. Congress, House of Representatives, Committee on Ways and Means, *1975 Annual Report of the Board of Trustees of the Federal Old-Age and Survivors Insurance and Disability Insurance Trust Funds*, 94th Congress, 1st session, May 6, 1975, p. 50.

system, the increasing ratio would mean an increasing burden on workers in providing the financial support of OASI beneficiaries.

The coming explosion in the OASI component of the social security system, however, is only barely suggested by projections of the increase in the number of OASI beneficiaries. Far more dramatic are the prospective increases in the amounts of benefits, and in the payroll or other taxes required to finance them.

Based on existing statutory provisions and on certain projections of basic demographic trends, the labor force, the unemployment rate, nominal wage rates, and changes in the consumer price index,[43] average annual retirement benefits will increase to $15,206 in the year 2000, to $77,431 in the year 2025, and to $366,258 in the year 2050. The average annual OASI payment to primary beneficiaries will rise to $12,643 in 2000, to $65,014 in 2025, and to $312,401 in 2050. In the year 2050 average benefits awarded would, from these projections, equal 38.6 percent of the average annual wage.

Startling as the prospective OASI benefits may appear, the estimated rate of increase is relatively modest—at least in comparison

[43] The specific demographic and economic assumptions for the years 1981-2049 are: (1) nominal wages per employee increase at an average annual rate of 6 percent; (2) the consumer price index increases at an average annual rate of 4 percent; (3) the number of covered workers (counting as separate workers those who have more than one job) increases from 98.4 million in 1975 to 130.4 million in 2025 (average annual rate of increase 1.1 percent) and to 144.7 million in 2050 (average annual rate of increase 0.4 percent); (4) unemployment averages 5 percent of the labor force; and (5) the fertility rate is 1.7 in 1977, increasing to 2.1 by 2005.

with that of the period 1950–1975 when OASI payments per beneficiary (primary and others) increased at an average annual rate of 8.5 percent. The projected growth in benefits from 1975 through 2050 is less—6.7 percent. It is not, therefore, the projected dollar increase in benefits that is the major source of concern about the future of OASI. Indeed, the rate of growth described above might well be taken as a measure of the success of the 1972–1973 legislation in systematizing and thereby moderating the expansion of benefits. If the projected benefit growth were to occur in an economic context marked by expansion of the labor force, employment, and nominal wages at the rate of the past twenty-five years, this expansion would have no more severe implications for the future than it has had to date. This is not to minimize the past consequences and certainly not to urge complacency about the effects of the projected growth. But the principal cause for concern lies in the financing of these future benefits.

OASI disbursements as a fraction of taxable payrolls are projected to decrease from 1975 through 1985, then to rise at a rapidly escalating rate.[44] In 1975, the OASI expenditure to taxable payroll ratio was estimated to be about 9.52 percent, which would decline to 9.24 percent in 1985 on the assumption that taxable payrolls will rise more rapidly (9.6 percent a year) than benefits (9.25 percent a year) over the next decade. Thereafter the increase in expenditures will outpace payroll growth. From 1985 to 2000, OASI expenditures are expected to increase at an average annual rate of about 7 percent while taxable payrolls expand by about 6.8 percent; the expenditure to taxable payroll ratio increases from 9.24 percent to 9.5 percent. From 2000 to 2025, expenditures grow at 8.7 percent a year in contrast to 6.2 percent for taxable payrolls and the expenditure to taxable payroll ratio jumps to 16.74 percent. The ratio will increase more modestly in the period 2025–2050, reaching 18.51 percent. This reflects a rise in expenditures at 6.7 percent a year while taxable payrolls grow at 6.2 percent.

Throughout the projection period the scheduled tax rates are less than the expected ratio of expenditures to taxable payroll, resulting in a shortfall that increases at an accelerating rate after 1985. In the year 2000, the scheduled tax rate is a full percentage point less than the projected expenditure to taxable payroll ratio. The difference increases to 6.5 percentage points in 2025 and to 8.3 percentage points in 2050. This means the annual deficit will increase from $10

[44] Expenditures are the sum of benefit payments and administration costs, averaging in the recent past about 1.6 percent of benefits.

billion in 1985 to $41.4 billion in the year 2000, to $1,226.8 billion in 2025, and to $7,033.3 billion in 2050.

If these deficits were to be eliminated by increasing OASI payroll tax rates rather than by expanding the payroll tax base (beyond what is expected under the automatic adjustment provisions), the required tax rate increases above those flowing from existing statutory provisions would be as shown in Table 19. (Compared with the 1975 OASI tax rate, the projected deficits would require an increase of 7.99 percent by 2025 and 9.76 percent by the year 2050.)

As indicated earlier, these estimates are functions of changes in the consumer price index, in nominal wages, in the population and its age distribution, and in the labor force and unemployment rate. Modest changes in the assumed values of one or more of these variables may result in relatively substantial changes in projected results.

One comparative measure of results based on alternative assumptions is the so-called "average-current-cost," defined as the

Table 19

INCREASE IN OASI TAXES UNDER EXISTING STATUTORY PROVISIONS NECESSARY TO FUND THE PROJECTED DEFICIT

(percent of taxable payroll)

Calendar Year	Schedule of OASI Tax Rates	Rates Required to Fund Expenditures	Increase in OASI Tax Rates over Scheduled Rates
1985	8.6	9.24	.64
1990	8.5	9.28	.78
1995	8.5	9.49	.99
2000	8.5	9.50	1.00
2005	8.5	9.81	1.31
2010	8.5	10.77	2.27
2015	10.2	12.44	2.24
2020	10.2	14.58	4.38
2025	10.2	16.74	6.54
2030	10.2	18.15	7.95
2035	10.2	18.61	8.41
2040	10.2	18.41	8.31
2045	10.2	18.26	8.06
2050	10.2	18.51	8.31

Source: U.S. Congress, House of Representatives, Committee on Ways and Means, *1975 Annual Report of the Board of Trustees of the Federal Old-Age and Survivors Insurance and Disability Insurance Trust Funds*, 94th Congress, 1st session, May 6, 1975.

arithmetic mean of OASI expenditures as a percent of taxable payrolls over the projection period.[45] Given the same basic assumptions as above, the average current cost of the OASI system for the twenty-five years from 1975 to 2000 is 11.42 percent, rising to 13.5 percent for the fifty years to 2025, and to 16.26 percent for the seventy-five years to 2050. With the same demographic, labor force, and employment assumptions and the same 4 percent per annum increase in the consumer price index, but assuming a 1.5 percent instead of 2 percent rate of increase in real wage rates, the corresponding average current costs become 11.95 percent, 14.83 percent, and 18.59 percent.[46] A one-half percentage point decrease in the assumed rate of productivity increase, in other words, inflates the average current cost over the seventy-five-year period about 2⅓ percentage points.

Under the same economic assumptions as in the basic projection, changes in demography would also influence projected results substantially. For example, if the fertility rate remains at 1.7 (the rate assumed for the year 1977) instead of rising to 2.1 in 2005 and thereafter, the average current cost goes from the projected 16.26 percent to 17.72 percent over the seventy-five-year period.

Differences in average current costs under several alternative assumptions are summarized in Table 20.[47]

Substantial reservations should be attached to these projections and to the differences among them with respect to differing economic and demographic assumptions.

Perhaps the most fragile assumption upon which the projections are based is that the consumer price index will continue to increase at rates substantially higher than those which have prevailed except in the very recent past. From 1900 through 1975, the average rate of advance of the consumer price index was 2.2 percent a year. While the 4 percent a year increase assumed in the standard projection may seem modest by comparison with the more recent experience, it is almost double the average rate which has more generally characterized U.S. economic experience. The assumed 4 percent rate need not be viewed as a conservative estimate of future price level

[45] For this purpose, expenditures include the cost of increasing the trust fund to an amount equal to one year's benefits plus administrative expenses by the end of the period.

[46] For a more extensive discussion of the differences in projected results, see U.S. Congress, House of Representatives, Committee on Ways and Means, *1975 Annual Report of the Board of Trustees of the Federal Old-Age and Survivors Insurance and Disability Insurance Trust Funds*, Appendix A, 94th Congress, 1st session, May 6, 1975, pp. 47-56.

[47] Ibid.

Table 20

OASI EXPENDITURE AS A PERCENT OF TAXABLE PAYROLL

Economic Assumptions				
Rate of increase in nominal wages	Rate of increase in CPI	**25 Years 1975–2000**	**50 Years 1975–2025**	**75 Years 1975–2050**
7%	5%	11.47	14.10	17.68
6%	4%	11.42	13.50	16.26
5%	3%	11.39	12.93	14.93
5½%	4%	11.95	14.83	18.59
½%	4%	10.93	12.32	14.30
Demographic Assumptions				
Fertility Rate				
2.1		11.42	13.50	16.26
1.7		11.40	13.80	17.72
2.5		11.43	13.23	15.19

Source: U.S. Congress, House of Representatives, Committee on Ways and Means, *1975 Annual Report of the Board of Trustees of the Federal Old-Age and Survivors Insurance and Disability Insurance Trust Funds*, 94th Congress, 1st session, May 6, 1975.

advances; for projections extending seventy-five years into the future, it seems plausible to anticipate that public policies will be at least as successful in moderating inflation as they have been over much of this century to date. And differences in the assumed inflation rate powerfully affect the projections. To take an extreme case, we might assume a zero rate of increase in the consumer price index beyond 1976, while retaining the other economic and demographic assumptions in the standard projection. On this basis, the ratios of OASI expenditures to taxable payrolls in the years 2025 and 2050 are 15.9 percent and 14.8 percent, respectively, compared with 16.7 percent and 18.5 in the standard projection.

Apart from the fact that the projections are obviously quite sensitive to variance in the specific assumptions, caution is also called for because each alternative set of assumptions implicitly holds everything else equal. It should be obvious, however, that in reality these influences are interactive. For example, differences in fertility rates are likely to be associated with differences in the composition of output, hence in the sectoral allocation of the labor force and in the overall rate of productivity gain. Nor do the alternative projections take account of differences in their respective consequences for total saving and capital formation, hence for changes in real wage rates.

In short, these projections suffer the same indeterminacy that plagues all forecasts.

Notwithstanding the caveats that should be observed in relying on the apparent precision of the projections, the overall configuration of the results strongly suggests an intensification of the so-called "crowding out" of private saving by the social security system. Crowding out is seen by some experts as the direct replacement of private sources of retirement income by the projected expansion of OASI benefits in relation to preretirement income. In essence, this is the social security wealth effect formulated by Feldstein. Our alternative analysis examines the implications of projected growth with respect to workers' permanent income and the relative cost of saving and consumption.

Direct Crowding Out. The direct crowding-out effect of the prospective surge in social security derives from the concept of a target "replacement ratio," that is, a desired amount of retirement benefits defined as some fixed portion of the employee's preretirement wage. Presumably the targeted replacement ratio accords with workers' preferences as revealed by the portion of their current incomes they are willing to save for retirement. Since the payroll taxes they must pay currently are not directly determined by the annuities they will receive but rather by the amount of benefits the current annuitants receive, there is no reason to assume that the social security component of their overall saving accords with their preference. Treating payroll taxes as exogenous to their saving-consumption choices, workers will, it is hypothesized, adjust other saving out of disposable income to the amount of their payroll taxes and anticipated social security benefits. While these are perceived as separate variables, the direction of their impact on the preferred amount of other saving is the same.

Suppose, for example, workers target a 70 percent replacement ratio; that is, suppose workers want their retirement income, irrespective of source, to equal 70 percent of the income they expect to be earning at the time of their retirement. Suppose, further, that the social security retirement benefit schedule appears to call for annuity income equal to 60 percent of workers' preretirement earnings. Then, in this view, workers will seek to save enough privately, either on their own or through private pension plans, to provide additional retirement income equal to 10 percent of their anticipated preretirement income. If social security benefits were to escalate to 65 percent, then workers' private saving would decrease commensurately. If social security benefits were to rise to levels over the target ratio —say, to 80 percent of preretirement income—retirement saving would turn negative. In this circumstance workers might withdraw past private savings to increase current consumption.

The argument at this level of generality does not necessarily imply any seriously adverse effects on private pension fund growth. It is directed, rather, at the total personal saving rate. Even in the case of negative private saving for retirement, the argument does not preclude workers' liquidating past savings to finance higher levels of consumption while maintaining or even, indeed, increasing their private pension fund saving.

Specification of the argument to include the extent to which private pension plans are integrated with social security benefits does suggest an adverse impact on private pension plan growth, if social security benefits are scheduled or expected to increase in relation to a fixed replacement ratio. For example, suppose combined social security and private pension fund benefits, net of tax, are targeted to replace 80 percent of the worker's preretirement gross pay; suppose further that the social security benefits of the worker's spouse are half the worker's primary benefit and that the marginal tax rate on the worker's private pension fund benefit is expected to be 20 percent; finally, suppose that the worker's primary social security benefit equals 40 percent of his preretirement gross pay. Given his total social security benefits (60 percent), the worker's required private pension benefits to attain the targeted 80 percent replacement ratio is 25 percent of his gross pay at the time of retirement. Were the primary social security benefit to increase to 50 percent of preretirement gross pay, his required private pension benefits skid to only 6.25 percent of preretirement gross pay. When the primary social security benefit increases to 53⅓ percent or more of preretirement gross pay, the required pension fund benefit goes to zero.[48]

There are, clearly, a number of variables affecting the examples illustrated above, assuming that the concept of a target replacement ratio is an operational reality. One such variable, or set of variables, consists of the statutory provisions which specify social security benefits. Another set is the income and other economic variables which enter into the social security benefit formula. The most

[48] See Geoffrey N. Calvert, "New Realistic Projections of Social Security Benefits and Taxes: Their Impact on the Economy and on Future Private Pensions," an address before the American Pension Conference, New York, December 4, 1973, pp. 32 ff., for additional illustrations and discussion.

important determinant of "crowding out," however, is the target replacement ratio itself. If the target were not a fixed ratio of preretirement income, the effects on private retirement saving of any given increase in social security benefits would be ambiguous. A central question, therefore, about the displacement of private saving in general, and private pension fund saving in particular, by the future expansion of social security, is the validity of the target replacement ratio concept.

The origin of the replacement ratio concept can be traced to the tax-transfer, income-redistributive nature of the Old-Age and Survivors Insurance system. Since the benefits individuals receive are not directly related to the taxes they pay, and since the level of benefits and taxes has been adjusted only periodically by Congress, the replacement ratio became a measure of the reasonableness of the OASI system. The concept has been used both to justify raising benefits when these have lagged behind increases in nominal wage rates and to check the expansion of the system to avoid overburdening the current generation of employed workers. General acceptance of the replacement ratio fostered the notion of a targeted total replacement ratio constraining the amount of current income saved irrespective of the relative costs of alternative forms of saving and consumption.

The concept of a *fixed* target replacement ratio, indeed of any replacement ratio, as a function in the worker's current saving is highly questionable. It derives from the view that the consumption-saving choice is concerned merely with the individual's continuing allocation of consumption. Saving, in this construction, is no more than deferred consumption.

Any such life-cycle model implies that the individual's saving decision depends on his making quite precise estimates of his life expectancy as a basis for determining the most effective distribution of his consumption over time, limited, of course, by his accumulated wealth and by his expected income.[49] The less precise his life-expectancy estimates, the less precise would be his determination of the optimum amount of disposable income to reserve for his future consumption. The greater the variability in his estimates of his mean life expectancy, the less precise must be his target replacement ratio and the less important the ratio becomes in his saving-consumption choices.

If the target replacement ratio hypothesis afforded a reasonably correct description of saving behavior, one would expect to find its

[49] See Stigler, *The Theory of Price*, pp. 276 ff.

empirical substantiation in the fact that, with relatively few exceptions, people die without accumulated wealth. More precisely, one should find that positive wealth accumulations were concentrated among those dying before their mean life expectancy; those living beyond the actuarial mean, for the most part, should have negative wealth. Federal estate tax return data, however, suggest that, if anything, the reverse is true: the younger the decedent, the smaller is the average accumulation, while the amount of accumulated wealth increases more than proportionately with the age of the decedents.[50] Federal estate tax returns, to be sure, are a biased sample of decedents, excluding those with accumulations less than the $60,000 gross estate exemption. It does not follow, however, that the relationship between the percentage distributions of age at death and of wealth shown in estate tax returns is not representative of all decedents.

As additional empirical substantiation of the target replacement ratio concept, one should find that insurance policy proceeds, for the most part, closely approximate the amounts needed to provide for continuation of beneficiaries' consumption levels, given their remaining life expectancy. Moreover, the implied price elasticity of demand for life insurance would be positive, rather than negative as in the case of demand functions generally. That is to say, if the unit cost of the insurance were to rise, individuals would increase their total premium payments while maintaining their benefits, rather than decrease their coverage.

If available, these pieces of empirical "evidence" would in fact be merely illustrative of the more general analytical proposition that the elasticity of consumption with respect to permanent income is unity.[51] This is, indeed, a widely accepted proposition, stemming from the work by Milton Friedman and others on the nature of the consumption function. But paradoxically, the wide acceptance of the proposition depends on neglect—or unquestioning acceptance—of the premise on which it is based, that the sole motive for economic behavior is ultimately consumption. A less restrictive view allowing for the possibility of accumulation for its own sake or for reasons other than to consume more in the future than otherwise tends to invalidate life-cycle theories of consumption and saving. At the applied level, the broader view undermines the notion of a target

[50] See U.S. Treasury Department, Internal Revenue Service, *Statistics of Income—1972 Estate Tax Returns.*

[51] See Paul J. Taubman, "The Interest Elasticity of Savings, Income Taxes and the Permanent-Income Hypothesis," *Journal of Political Economy*, vol. 83, no. 1 (February 1975), pp. 215-218.

replacement ratio as a determinant of the individual's saving-consumption choice.

As suggested above, the question of the validity of the target replacement ratio concept is a critical matter in correctly evaluating the implications of varying rates of growth of social security for the private pension system. The prevailing consensus is that this concept is valid as a practical matter. Indeed, it has been expressed as an ethical criterion that presumably *should* guide public and private policy about retirement income provisions, not merely as a factor that influences personal decisions. Here, for instance, is the target ratio concept in an ethical content:

> But on one thing all are agreed. It makes no sense at all for a retired person who is making no contribution to the economy to receive *more* income for doing nothing than an actively employed person who is going to work every day. That does not mean that the common sense limit to pensions-plus-primary-Social-Security is 100% of gross pay at retirement. It means that: After-tax-pension *plus* primary-Social-Security, at the time of retirement, should not exceed say 80% of gross pay while working.[52]

If the target replacement ratio concept were sound, either analytically or as a characterization of actual economic behavior, then the prospective rapid growth of the social security system is likely not merely to challenge the growth but to threaten the continuing existence of the private pension system. "Crowding out" follows if *in fact* workers' saving propensities are tailored to a replacement ratio. In our analytical construction, however, any target replacement ratio would be an artificial and restrictive depiction of the saving function, the real determinants of which, we argue, are permanent income and the cost of saving relative to the cost of consumption. Given the level of permanent income, a reduction in the relative cost of saving results in an increase in the proportion of income currently saved. Other things being equal, this change in the uses of current income necessarily implies an increase in future income. Insofar as saving is responsive to changes in its relative cost, therefore, there is no necessary, fixed relationship between future and current income.

Conversely, if desired future income were fixed in relation to current income, then current saving must be completely unresponsive to changes in the relative costs of saving and consumption. But if this

[52] Calvert, "New Realistic Projections of Social Security Benefits and Taxes," p. 32.

were true, consumption, too, would have to be unresponsive to its relative cost. Suppose the target replacement ratio is specified in nominal rather than real terms: the assumed inelasticity of consumption with respect to its cost means that the worker's desired *real* replacement ratio is highly variable, or more precisely, that he would be indifferent about the real amount of his future consumption in making his current consumption-saving choice.[53] The strong pressures for cost-of-living adjustments in current or future retirement annuities are persuasive evidence against the notion that desired replacement ratios are specified in nominal rather than real terms. If on the other hand the desired replacement ratio is specified in real terms, the ratio measured in nominal terms would be highly variable. Putting the desired replacement ratio in nominal terms would depend on the target real replacement ratio and anticipated changes in the cost of consumption. Suppose the desired real replacement ratio were fixed: any change in cost anticipations would necessarily change the desired replacement ratio measured in nominal terms. In either case, the idea of a fixed replacement ratio as a major determinant of current consumption-saving choices appears to be highly implausible.

Since the notion of a fixed replacement ratio does not characterize a real determinant in workers' saving functions, it cannot be argued that an increase in social security benefits toward some preconceived target ratio necessarily constrains private saving. This is not to say that a prospective surge in social security benefits is without seriously adverse implications for private saving.

Given that workers' saving-consumption choices are not geared to some target replacement ratio, the question remains whether employers are constrained by an increase in the social security replacement ratio in offering private pension plan coverage and benefits. To conclude that they are would be plausible only if the increase in the social security replacement ratio, in itself, increased the cost to employers of providing pension benefits relative to wages and other compensation. It is difficult to perceive any such relationship. Accordingly, it is doubtful that any projected increase in the social security replacement ratio, in itself, need limit private pension plan provisions. Obviously, retirement income could very well exceed preretirement earnings, possibly by substantial amounts. One may further conclude that private pension fund policy need not be constrained by the prospect of rising replacement ratios. The attractiveness to employees of any given pension plan provision for retirement income depends on the

[53] Or that he anticipates either a zero or constant rate of change in the cost of consumption over his remaining life.

efficiency gains the plan affords, irrespective of the prevailing or prospective replacement ratio.

The Alternative Analysis of the Displacement of Private Saving by Social Security. An assessment of the effects of the long-term projections of social security depends on the associated changes in the cost of social security annuities relative to the cost of private claims to future income. Since any given increase in the replacement ratio may be associated with a wide range of changes in the relative costs of social security and private annuities, the projected replacement ratio has little evaluative relevance.

It was urged earlier in this discussion that substantial reservations should be attached to the various projections of social security costs and benefits. Moreover, inherent uncertainties preclude any confident forecast of likely changes in the cost of social security benefits relative to private annuities. The magnitude of the possible displacement of private provisions for retirement income by social security, accordingly, cannot be projected with any degree of precision.

To take an example in detail: on the basis of the demographic and economic assumptions of the standard projection, the cost of OASI annuities is estimated to fall modestly relative to that of privately supplied claims for retirement income, in contrast to experience from the early 1940s to date. To illustrate, consider a twenty-two-year-old male starting work in 1975 and contemplating retirement at age sixty-five in the year 2018. Assume that his earnings in 1975 are equal to the mean for his age and increase each year to equal the projected mean wage of thirty-four-year olds in the year 1987, rising thereafter at an average annual rate of 6 percent (estimated from a 2 percent per annum increase in productivity and a 4 percent per annum increase in the consumer price index). We use a 7 percent discount rate—roughly consistent with the CPI increase—to compute the present value of his payroll taxes and OASI benefits,[54] assuming the existing statutory provisions remain unaltered and dictate all adjustments in benefits and in payroll taxes automatically in response to changes in the consumer price index.

On these assumptions, the present value of his expected benefits is $37,347 while that of his projected payroll taxes is $33,234; his social security wealth is positive. The excess of the present value of his projected benefits over the present value of his payroll taxes means

[54] The amount of these benefits is determined by reference to the current estimates of his and his spouse's life expectancies beyond retirement at age sixty-five, as well as his projected earnings and the projected benefit schedules.

that the effective discount rate is greater than the 7 percent rate actually used. The cost of social security benefits, as projected, is consequently less than the cost of private retirement income claims.

These results are in contrast to the negative wealth computed for social security for most of the period since the program was established.[55] The projected shift to positive social security wealth implies a more substantial reduction in private purchases of retirement income claims in the future than in the past. In short, the assumptions upon which the standard projection of social security are based lead to the conclusion that the displacement of private saving by social security will intensify rather than abate over the next several generations.

However, the standard projection also shows increasing annual deficits in the social security accounts. These deficits will have to be eliminated by additional payroll or general taxes or in some other way. Although the method chosen to balance the annual account is certainly not inconsequential, the relative effects of the alternatives are likely to be less significant than the certainty that the deficit will be financed by additional withdrawals from the compensation of employees.[56]

If we assume that an increase in payroll tax rates closely approximates the required incremental burden on the average worker for financing the projected OASI benefits, the results will differ materially from those computed above. On this assumption, the present value of his payroll taxes will increase by slightly more than 10 percent, to $36,703. While his net social security wealth remains positive, it is reduced by 84 percent.

For the twenty-two-year-old labor-force entrant in 1985, the present value of his expected benefits is $63,088, as against the $61,537 present value of his payroll taxes under the existing schedules. If the payroll tax rate were increased just sufficiently to eliminate the deficit in the OASI accounts, the present value of his payroll taxes would rise to $73,427 and his social security wealth would be negative. For the twenty-two-year-old in the year 2000, social security wealth is negative whether the present value of his payroll taxes is computed from existing schedules or on the assumption that annual OASI expenditures are fully financed by payroll taxes.[57] While these

[55] See Appendix A, pp. 107-121.

[56] As between an explicit increase in payroll tax rates or financing the deficit out of additional general tax revenues, the difference in effective overall tax rate on the average worker is likely to be modest.

[57] These estimates are also based on a 7 percent discount rate which, as noted above, is consistent with the assumption of a 4 percent per annum increase in the consumer price index.

calculations show a shift to negative social security wealth beyond 1985, the present values of payroll taxes and of benefits are substantially closer in the above examples than in the case of a twenty-two-year-old starting work in 1970 or during most of the postwar period. This suggests a long-term trend toward increasing displacement of private retirement saving by social security.

While the displacement effect of social security is likely to intensify in the foreseeable future, it does not follow that this effect will fall as severely on private pension funds as on other private saving. One of the principal factors in the projected displacement is the assumed 4 percent per annum increase in the consumer price index, reflecting a high inflation rate by the standard of U.S. experience. Given that the forecast is reasonable, inflation of such magnitude necessarily implies a long-term tendency for effective federal income tax rates to increase.[58] This in turn implies an increase in the efficiency gains provided by private pension plans if they continue to receive the same tax treatment. While aggregate private saving may well be less than it would have been in the absence of the projected social security changes, it does not follow that private pension fund saving would be equally or even significantly affected so long as it continues to offer efficiency gains.

The differences between these analyses of the displacement of private saving by social security are of more than abstract interest. Both analyses drive to the same general conclusion, that the expected rapid growth in social security will depress the rate of private saving. The view that the extent of displacement depends on the change in the replacement ratio, we have seen, is highly constrictive and mechanistic. It ignores the effects of a shift in demand for privately supplied claims to future income because of changes in the relative cost of saving, and it arbitrarily ties private pension fund provisions directly to the OASI replacement ratio.[59]

[58] This conclusion must hold for the long run whether or not some sort of indexing is adopted in the federal income tax, unless the rate of increase in real federal expenditures is slowed. Some proponents of indexing the increase in nominal income attributable to inflation out of the income tax base maintain that the resulting slower rate of increase in federal tax revenues will inhibit the increase in federal spending. If this assumption were not to prove correct, effective rates of taxes on labor income would rise in the long run.

[59] Calvert, "New Realistic Projections of Social Security Benefits and Taxes." As noted above, even if the replacement ratio were *the* determinant of private provision for retirement income, it does not necessarily follow that private pension plans would be affected in the same degree as total private saving by any given increase in the replacement ratio.

The alternative analysis presented here examines the projected growth of social security to ascertain the cost of OASI benefits relative to the cost of private provisions. But since the cost of privately supplied retirement income is not a function of the observed or projected OASI replacement ratio at any given time, changes in this ratio are not pertinent per se to the determination of whether social security expansion will more or less severely depress the private saving rate. That determination, to repeat, depends on (1) the change in the cost of OASI benefits relative to privately supplied future income claims associated with the projected growth, and (2) the market adjustment of the relative costs of saving and consumption and in particular the magnitude of the saving response to the adjustment process. In this construction, as our illustrations seek to show, growth in the social security system at the rates given in the standard projection implies greater displacement of overall private saving. The future growth of private pension plans, however, need not necessarily be retarded by OASI expansion, provided that private plans remain able to offer workers efficiency gains for their retirement saving.

Pension Reform Legislation of 1974. Potentially far more consequential than OASI expansion to the development of the private pension system is the Employees' Retirement Income Security Act of 1974 (ERISA). This legislation was aimed at eliminating alleged abuses and improvident management in private plans, thereby more fully securing employees' rights to pension benefits.

The background for the legislation is discussed in a report of the Senate Committee on Labor and Public Welfare.[60] The report cites a staff study showing that since 1950, on the basis of a sample of 1,500 plans with 14 million participants, the number of workers who did *not* receive pension benefits or vested rights thereto exceeded those who did. Another study cited in the committee report found that the median retirement benefit for normal, early, and disability retirement paid by private plans in 1969 and 1970 was less than $100 per month.

The committee report focused on what it deemed the stringency of requirements for the receipt of private pension benefits, the inadequacy of plan funding in some cases, and the deficiencies in plan investment policies and fiduciary responsibility. In summary, it found that:

[60] U.S. Congress, Senate, Committee on Labor and Public Welfare, *Retirement Security for Employees Act of 1972*, No. 92-1150, 92nd Congress, 2nd session, September 18, 1972.

(1) Approximately one-third of the pension plans studied had both a minimum age and service requirement for participation in a pension plan. An additional 25 percent had a minimum service requirement only and approximately 35 percent of the plans had no age or service requirements for eligibility to participate.

(2) The most common normal retirement age was sixty-five (occurring in almost 90 percent of the plans). In over half of these plans, a service requirement also existed, in a few cases as much as thirty years. In the case of over one-fourth of all participants, attainment of age sixty-five and at least fifteen years of service was required for a normal retirement benefit.

(3) About 13 percent of the plans studied did not provide for any vesting at all. For those plans which had vesting provisions expressed as a combination of age and service, the combinations most frequently encountered were in the range of from forty to forty-four years of age with from fifteen to nineteen years of service. However, more stringent vesting formulas were also encountered; 8 percent of the plans had both an age and a service vesting qualification which required at least age fifty and twenty years of service for a vesting right. In the plans where only a service requirement was established for vesting, over one-fourth of these plans required more than fifteen years of service to qualify. Among pension plans containing vesting provisions, over 55 percent had only a service requirement.

(4) Over 30 percent of private pension plans were utilizing a deferred graded form of vesting, by which a certain percentage of a participant's accrued retirement benefit is vested initially, and the percentage increases periodically as the employee completes additional service. Profit-sharing plans utilize this type of vesting more frequently (over three-fourths of all such plans).

(5) Information regarding the assets and liabilities of pension plans was reported inconsistently and incompletely by a sizable number of pension plans. However, of those plans which did report appropriately, over 45 percent had a ratio of assets (valued at market) to total liabilities of over 75 percent, and three-fourths of the plans had a ratio of assets (valued at market) to vested liabilities of over 75 percent. While this finding established that a majority of pension

funds are generally well funded, the responses also revealed a significant minority of plans which were substantially underfunded. Over 10 percent of the plans reporting disclosed a ratio of assets (valued at market) to vested liabilities of 50 percent or less.

(6) Only 40 percent of private pension plans had formal restrictions pertaining to investment of pension plan assets, and less than one-half of all plans required annual audits by an independent licensed or certified public accountant.

(7) Over 35 percent of the pension plans studied, covering a similar number of participants, did not provide an opportunity for participants to request a hearing on claims; less than 30 percent of all plans provided for a written denial of such claims; and only 30 percent of all plans provided for review procedures with respect to denial of claims.[61]

Treasury data showed that there were 1,227 plans terminated in 1972. Of these, 546 terminations resulted in losses totaling $49 million (present value) of benefits for 19,400 participants, whose average loss was $2,500. These participants comprised 0.08 percent of workers covered in 1972 by private pension plans.[62]

Such were the data upon which the Congress determined that there was an urgent need to enact pension reform legislation. Whether the data were representative of the private pension system as a whole cannot be definitively established. Surely the extent of "inadequate" funding cited for trusteed plans substantially overstated the case for insured plans, which represent an increasing fraction of participating employees. Indeed, the "inadequacy" of the funding is merely a function of the degree of vesting that is deemed to be "correct." While funding provisions may be subject to public regulation, there is no justification in economic analysis for determining "correct" levels, any more than there is analytical justification for a public policy determination of the "correct" amount of any other component of employees' compensation.[63]

The pertinent question is whether the legislation will have the results desired or whether it will in fact aggravate the deficiencies the act was intended to correct. Suppose that the effect of the new requirements imposed by ERISA proves to be some substantial re-

---

[61] Ibid.

[62] U.S. Congress, Senate, Committee on Finance, *Private Pension Plan Reform*, Report on S. 1179, 93rd Congress, 2nd session, August 23, 1973.

[63] See note 23 above.

tardation in the growth of private pension plans. It certainly may be argued that the greater welfare of workers whose pension benefits have been enhanced would be partly or wholly offset by the loss of welfare for those workers who, because of the legislation, are never covered by a plan.

ERISA is likely to slow the growth of private pension plans to the extent that it erodes the efficiency gains the plans have afforded in the past. The major provisions of the act—those pertaining to vesting, funding, plan termination insurance, and fiduciary responsibility—increase the cost of providing any given level of pension benefits and impede the capacity of private plans to extend efficiency gains to their participants. While these provisions will affect the operation of all existing pension plans, they are likely to weigh most heavily on the self-insured, or trusteed pension plans. The provisions pertaining to H.R. 10 (Keogh) plans and to individual retirement accounts, on the other hand, tend to extend the opportunity for individuals to realize efficiency gains.

Vesting. One of the principal rationales for ERISA was the allegedly worrisome extent to which workers covered by private pension plans failed to receive benefits when they retired from active, full-time employment. While a variety of circumstances explaining such cases could be cited, the lack of plan provision for full—or substantially full—vesting of benefit rights was advanced as a major factor. A central aim of the legislation, therefore, was to establish formal vesting requirements for noncontributory plans.

ERISA establishes three alternative rules for vesting an employee's rights in the benefits accrued from his employer's contributions. The "five-to-fifteen-year rule" requires that the employee must be at least 25 percent vested in his accrued benefits after five years of covered service, with this percentage increased for each year of service thereafter to achieve 100 percent vesting after fifteen years of service. The schedule delineated in the statute is:

Years of service	*Nonforfeitable percentage*
5	25
6	30
7	35
8	40
9	45
10	50
11	60

Years of service	*Nonforfeitable percentage*
12	70
13	80
14	90
15 and thereafter	100

In lieu of following this graduated vesting schedule, the "ten-year-rule" allows a plan to provide that an employee's accrued benefits will be 100 percent vested after ten years of covered service.

Finally, the "rule of forty-five" requires that an employee with five or more years of covered service must be at least 50 percent vested in his accrued benefits when the sum of his age and years of covered service totals forty-five. Each year thereafter the percentage of his benefits which must be vested in him increases according to the following schedule:

Years of service equal or exceed	*Sum of age and service equals or exceeds*	*Nonforfeitable percentage*
5	45	50
6	47	60
7	49	70
8	51	80
9	53	90
10	55	100

Under this rule, the benefits of an employee with ten years of service must, in every case, be at least 50 percent vested and an additional 10 percent must become nonforfeitable with each additional year of service.

In addition to these vesting rules, the legislation broadened the mandated employee benefits. Particularly important is the requirement that a plan provide benefits for the covered employee's surviving spouse equal to at least half the amount paid to the participant during their joint lives.

Implementation of these rules by the plan clearly requires the maintenance of records about each employee, and this requirement is made explicit in the statute.

The unit cost impact of the new benefit and vesting requirements cannot be precisely quantified because of the great variety in pension plan provisions at the time of the change in the law. However, some indication of the range of cost increases was provided by Donald S. Grubbs, Jr., in a study prepared for the Joint Committee on Internal

Revenue Taxation in 1973.[64] Grubbs estimated cost increases for a number of vesting proposals under various assumptions with respect to the then-present extent of vesting for 469 trusteed pension plans. While the proposals Grubbs examined differ in detail from the changes later enacted, some of his findings offer a reasonably close approximation of the cost impact of the actual statutory provisions.

Grubbs estimated that for those plans with no vesting provisions, then accounting for 23 percent of the total pension plan participants, 100 percent vesting at ten years would increase plan costs by between 0.2 and 0.6 percent of payroll and between 3.0 and 26.0 percent of existing plan costs. A rule-of-fifty vesting requirement would increase these plans' costs by almost the same amounts, from 0.2 to 0.7 percent of payroll and from 3.0 to 28.0 percent of present plan costs.

For plans with some vesting provisions, but less liberal than those proposed, the range of cost increases for 100 percent vesting at ten years would be 0 to 0.2 percent of payroll and 0 to 7.0 percent of present plan costs. The corresponding cost increases under a "rule of fifty" for such plans, which cover 56 percent of all participants, would be 0 to 0.3 percent and 0 to 12.0 percent. The plans characterized as having liberal vesting provisions, accounting for 21 percent of all participants, would have no increase in costs under full vesting at ten years, but would experience additional costs under the "rule of fifty," ranging up to 0.2 percent of payroll and up to 7.0 percent of present plan costs.

Funding. Another of the major policy concerns to which ERISA was directed was inadequacy of pension plan funding. The data provided the Senate Committee on Labor and Public Welfare do not suggest that this was a widespread problem. Indeed, the committee's report took note of the fact that the majority of pension plans were well funded. This conclusion was based, at least in substantial part, on a sample of 469 trustee-administered plans with 7,100,205 participants. As shown in Table 21, almost one-fifth of the plans had assets, measured in current market value, equal to 100 percent or more of the present value of total accrued retirement benefits. Moreover, for 45 percent of the plans, the ratio exceeded 75 percent. Relating assets to vested liabilities, over three-fourths of the surveyed plans had ratios in excess of 75 percent.

The committee noted, however, that a significant number of plans were substantially underfunded with asset-liability ratios of

[64] Donald S. Grubbs, Jr., "The Cost of Mandatory Vesting Provisions," a study prepared for the Joint Committee on Internal Revenue Taxation, July 30, 1973.

Table 21

ASSETS AT MARKET VALUE AS A PERCENT OF PRESENT VALUE OF TOTAL ACCRUED RETIREMENT BENEFITS

Assets as Percent of Accrued Benefits	**By Plan**		**By Participant**	
	Number	Percent	Number	Percent
25% or less	33	7	541,801	8
26–50%	118	25	1,798,945	25
51–75%	104	22	2,134,601	30
76–100%	117	25	1,211,298	17
101–125%	55	12	949,975	13
126–150%	20	4	134,252	2
151–175%	8	2	52,498	1
Over 175%	14	3	276,835	4
Total	469	100	7,100,205	100

Source: U.S. Congress, Senate, Committee on Labor and Public Welfare, *Retirement Security for Employees Act of 1972*, No. 92-1150, 92nd Congress, 2nd session, September 18, 1972, page 97.

50 percent or less. Also weighing heavily in consideration of funding adequacy were the unhappy experiences of employees in certain plans.[65]

Before the enactment of ERISA, pension plans were required to make irrevocable allocations to a trust, or to purchase insurance contracts, at least sufficient to pay the normal pension costs plus interest on unfunded liabilities attributable to the past service of covered employees. This requirement was deemed inadequate by proponents of ERISA because it was designed to prevent any increase in unfunded liabilities but not to reduce them.

ERISA requires employers with defined benefit plans to contribute annually an amount not less than the total normal cost of funding the plan plus amortization of unfunded past-service costs, increases in liabilities and experience losses, minus amortization of reductions in pension liabilities and experience gains. Initial past-service costs of new plans, under these requirements, may be amor-

[65] Nowhere in the committee's reports is there provided any discussion of the concept of funding adequacy or of the criteria which should be used in assessing the adequacy of any plan's funding. Interpretation of the data on fund assets in relation to liabilities presented in the committee's reports, accordingly, is ambiguous, and the reports' assertions on the matter of adequacy appear to be highly arbitrary.

tized over a period no longer than thirty years; past-service liabilities of plans in existence at the beginning of 1974 may be amortized over a maximum of forty years; and experience gains and losses are to be amortized over a maximum of fifteen years. Amortization payments must cover both principal and interest. If the employer fails to meet these funding standards, an excise tax is imposed equal to 5 percent of the funding deficiency at the end of each plan year. If the deficiency is not corrected within the period allowed after notice by the Internal Revenue Service, an additional tax is imposed equal to 100 percent of the deficiency.

The hardship that these funding requirements impose on some employers was recognized in ERISA, which allows waivers by the Internal Revenue Service on a year-by-year basis under certain conditions. The IRS will consider such factors as an employer operating at a loss, substantial unemployment in the employer's trade or business, depressed sales and profits in the employer's industry, and whether the employer will continue his plan only if the funding requirement is waived. These waiver provisions obviously pertain only to relatively extreme hardships caused by the funding requirements. They afford no relief for a broad range of circumstances in which employers would want to terminate their plans unless the additional costs imposed by the funding requirements could be offset by reductions in employee compensation.

Unfortunately, there are no reliable data available for estimating the increase in plan costs imposed by the new funding requirements. The funding provisions would tend to increase costs for a substantial number of plans even had ERISA not also required greater vesting. The conjoined effect of the new vesting and funding rules must magnify the cost impact on plans deficient by ERISA standards.

Termination Insurance. To avert any loss of employee benefits through terminations, ERISA requires pension plans to obtain termination insurance. To administer these provisions, the act created a new agency, the Pension Benefit Guaranty Corporation, in the Department of Labor. Single-employer plans must pay a premium of $1.00 per participant and multi-employer plans pay $0.50. In later years a plan may choose a premium schedule based on its unfunded insurance benefits and its total insured benefits. In the event a plan is terminated, its beneficiaries would receive insurance payments not exceeding the actuarial equivalent of the lesser of 100 percent of average wages during the individual's five highest-paid years of plan participation or $750 per month. These limits, however, will be raised in proportion to future increases in the social security contribution and benefit base. In the event of plan termination, the employer, if solvent, is liable to reimburse the Pension Benefit Guaranty Corporation for its insurance payments, although the extent of this liability is limited to 30 percent of his net worth.

Even more than in the case of the new funding provisions, the termination insurance provisions appear to address the exceptions rather than the rule. The meager evidence available suggests that, in general, terminations without substantial recovery of benefits by participants were experienced by a very small fraction of plans, covering a very limited number of beneficiaries, and involving relatively small losses. The overall incidence of these losses should be perceived as unavoidable in terms of market risk and all but inconsequential in relation to the common risks of income loss from unemployment, injury, or sickness.

To be sure, the incremental cost to the employer represented by the insurance premium he is required to pay also appears to be inconsequential. The more significant increase in pension plan cost derives from the liability to reimburse the PBGC for payments to participants and beneficiaries if the plan is terminated. The present value of this contingent liability, even appropriately adjusted by the employer's assessment that termination is unlikely, may in many cases substantially exceed the present value of the amount of premium payments required over the life of the plan.

Fiduciary Responsibility. Another of the major legislative concerns ERISA addressed was the improvement of standards for pension fund administration and correction of the infrequent but attention-getting mishandling of pension fund assets. To this end ERISA establishes a complex set of rules governing the conduct and operations of plan fiduciaries, including not only those officially designated as plan administrators but others, like corporate executives, who because of their position affecting the administration of the plan might be held liable for them.

The new law imposes all the usual requirements on fiduciaries—for example, that they discharge their duties solely in the interests of the participants and beneficiaries of the plan and that, when making investment decisions, they follow the "prudent man rule" and diversify the assets of the plan to minimize the risk of loss. Except for profit-sharing, stock bonus, thrift and other savings plans expressly designed to invest in the securities of the employer, pension plans generally can invest a maximum of 10 percent of plan assets in the employer's securities.

The law delineates quite specifically all party-in-interest transactions and other prohibited transactions, for instance, a fiduciary dealing with the plan assets for his own account, and penalizes them with substantial excise taxes (5 percent initially, then 100 percent of the amount of the transaction). The individual engaging in the prohibited transaction is disqualified as a fiduciary.

ERISA also prescribes elaborate reporting and disclosure rules. The plan administrator is required to publish a comprehensive description of the plan and a summary description, a copy of which must be provided each of the plan's participants. The summary description must be written plainly enough to assure that the average plan participant will understand it. It must include all basic information about eligibility for participation and benefit vesting; conditions which disqualify a participant from receiving benefits; plan funding and financing and identification of the organization through which benefits are paid; and claims procedures and remedies available if a claim is rejected.

The most severe aspect of this section is the provision that holds fiduciaries civilly liable for both losses to the plan and the profits made through the use of plan assets. Exculpatory agreements once used by trustees as protection against legal action are voided by ERISA, but the fiduciary is permitted to purchase insurance to cover his potential liability. In effect, these provisions, in conjunction with those pertaining to funding adequacy, impose the risk of financial market adversity on plan administrators and company officials. The effect of the rules is to increase costs for the plans, either in the form of fiduciary insurance or as a result of unduly conservative investment policies. Since ERISA permits bonds and other fixed-income securities to be valued at cost, no capital loss need be recognized in the annual calculation of experience gains and losses unless the securities are sold. By shifting the composition of fund assets more toward bonds, fiduciaries can minimize their personal liability and the risk of law suits. While market conditions may periodically warrant a compositional shift toward fixed-income securities, permanent statutory pressure for such a portfolio clearly tends toward less-than-optimal diversification of pension fund assets, reducing yields to less than those realized over the past two decades. Any such artificial constraint on the diversification of fund portfolios will impair one of the major elements in the efficiency gains supplied by private pension plans.

Individual Retirement Accounts and Keogh Plans. ERISA substantially raised the limits on deductions for self-employed individuals' contributions to Keogh plans. Where formerly the maximum deductible contribution was the lesser of $2,500 or 10 percent of earned income, deductions of the lesser of $7,500 or 15 percent are now permitted. Defined benefit plans were also authorized for the self-employed, if the plans adhere to guideline benefit schedules. While antidiscrimination rules and tax penalties on excess contributions and premature distributions were also enacted, the substantial increase in the allowable contribution will tend to increase the amount of retirement saving by the self-employed and their employees.

In recognition of the fact that many employees are not covered by retirement plans, and in an effort to give these employees equal standing with those participating in employer-financed retirement plans and with self-employed individuals, ERISA authorizes individual retirement accounts for these persons. More specifically, the act permits a deduction for amounts set aside, either by the employee or on his behalf by his employer, in an IRA or an equivalent purchase of retirement bonds. The deduction is limited to the lesser of $1,500 or 15 percent of the employee's compensation. The investment income of the IRA is exempt from tax as it is earned. All of the distributions from the IRA to the individual are taxed as ordinary income; if the distributions are made prematurely, that is, if the individual is not at least 59½ years of age or disabled, an additional penalty tax of 10 percent is imposed. Distributions are not eligible for capital gains treatment, nor for the special averaging rules which apply to lump-sum disbursements. The general income-averaging rules do apply, however. If they meet the other requirements, IRA distributions are eligible for the retirement income credit.

The full amount of IRA funds must be distributed by age 70½. Until then distributions may be made in the form of an annuity, the minimum amount of which is based on the remaining expected life of the individual or the remaining joint lifetime of the individual and spouse; or by payment of equal annual amounts over some specified number of years not in excess of the individual's life expectancy (or the joint life expectancy of the individual and spouse). Where the distribution falls short of the minimum amount, a 50 percent penalty tax is imposed on the shortfall.

Significant constraints are imposed on IRAs, in addition to the limitation on the amount of deductible annual contribution. An IRA may be established as a domestic trust or as a custodial account; the trustee generally is a bank or some other organization with trust administration capability. While the trust assets may not be commingled with other property, the IRA may participate in a common trust fund. There are, accordingly, few limitations on the types of assets in which the trust may be invested or on the types of financial organizations that may make IRA accounts available. One such limitation is that life insurance contracts generally are not eligible; only annuity contracts and endowments specifically restricted to provide retirement insurance are authorized. The trust assets are nontransferable and may not be posted by the individual as collateral. Similarly, the individual is barred from certain transactions with the account; for example, he may not borrow from it. If he engages in a prohibited transaction with his account, the account ceases to be a qualified IRA as of the beginning of the year in which the transaction occurred. The market value of all the assets in the account is treated as if they had been distributed to him, and this amount is taxed as ordinary income.

Notwithstanding these constraints, the IRA affords the individual a highly flexible tax-sheltered vehicle for saving for retirement. The range of eligible trust arrangements and assets permits him to diversify his retirement saving as he prefers. For most employees the permissible annual contribution significantly exceeds the per-employee amounts contributed by employers to pension plans. By their very nature IRAs are fully vested in the individual and completely portable.

In short, the IRA offers the individual the opportunity to realize virtually all the efficiency gains provided by employers' pension plans and, indeed, provides some advantages over the latter. The single exception is that the individual must incur information and transaction costs that are now assumed by employers and spread over the pension costs of all covered employees. If the employer provides IRAs for his employees in lieu of a pension plan, even this element of efficiency gain may be matched.

The IRA provisions of ERISA, taken by themselves, must be seen as substantially reducing, if not entirely eliminating, the cost advantage of saving through an employer-sponsored pension plan, as against the worker's own provisions for retirement income. The availability of IRAs thus significantly enlarges the scope of traditional pension plans and diversifies the range of retirement income claims available to individual workers. With any significant cross-elasticity of demand for pension saving, other things being equal, the availability of IRAs might substantially reduce worker demand for pension plan coverage of the traditional configuration.

Other things, however, are not equal. Other provisions of ERISA enhance the value of pension plan saving to participating workers. The change in vesting and funding requirements, plan termination insurance, and the new rules pertaining to fiduciary responsibility, eventually, if not immediately, must be perceived by workers as significantly increasing the risk-adjusted present worth of the pension plan benefits at any given level of forgone current wage. The net effect of this on pension plan growth is ambiguous. ERISA, taken in sum, reduces the cost to workers of purchasing claims for retirement income. Aggregate saving for retirement is therefore likely to increase at a more rapid rate than otherwise. The composition of this saving, however, is also likely to shift—away from employer pension plans and toward IRAs.

The increases initiated by ERISA in the present value of pension benefits, or equivalently, the reductions in the cost of acquiring retirement income, cannot be construed as a free lunch for employees. They are offset by equal increases in the pension plan costs to employers. These increased costs must ultimately be deducted from the increased levels of employee compensation that employers would otherwise provide. The cost increases should therefore be construed as the outer limits on the substitution of the present value of retirement income for current wage or salary income. To illustrate, consider the effects of the change in vesting requirements.

Assume that, in a non-ERISA context, an employer has 100 employees covered by a benefit-determined retirement plan that will pay the employee $4,000 per year upon his retirement. To simplify the illustration, ignore survivorship benefits and assume that the primary beneficiary will live ten years after retirement. For each employee who will eventually receive the retirement benefits, about $28,000 must be accumulated by the time of retirement, figuring on a 7 percent discount rate. Assume further that, on the basis of past experience, only one employee in ten will actually qualify for retirement benefits and that both the employer and the employees are equally informed as to this actuarial likelihood. The employer each year would then allocate to the pension fund the amount necessary to accumulate $280,000 ($28,000 each for ten employees) over, say, an average of thirty remaining working years for his employees. At an interest rate of 7 percent, the employer must pay into the trust fund $298 per year for each of the ten annuities he expects eventually will be paid, or a total annual contribution of $2,980. Assuming the employee discount rate is also 7 percent, each employee perceives the annual contribution to be worth $29.80 to him ($2,980 divided by 100 employees), or equivalently, he may perceive that he has a one in ten chance of receiving an annuity which costs $298 per year for thirty years. In agreeing to these pension plan provisions, the worker necessarily accepts his employer's $29.80 contribution as compensation in the form of retirement income claims, hence agrees to forgo $29.80 per year of current wage or salary.

In contrast, suppose that the employer is required to vest every one of his 100 employees in the pension plan's benefits. His annual cost to provide a $4,000 annuity for each of the 100 employees increases tenfold, to $29,800. The annual value of pension benefits now increases from $29.80 to $298.00 per employee. Clearly, unless the employees' productivity has increased equivalently, the employer will not be able or willing to incur this additional compensation cost per worker. He will seek, instead, to substitute the additional $26,820 of pension plan costs for current wage and salary or other compensation or to defer increases in compensation to the same effect.

As indicated, workers certainly are likely to perceive the increase in value of their prospective pension plan benefits attributable to 100 percent vesting. Since this reduces the cost to them of acquiring retirement income, they should be willing to give up some current consumption for the additional retirement income, hence are likely to accept some substitution of additional employer contributions to the pension plan for current compensation.[66] It does not follow, however, that workers would be willing fully to substitute the increase in the present value of their pension plan benefits for current compensation. The extent of any such substitution is determined by their saving functions, hence by their cross-elasticities of demand for future income and current consumption and for alternative types of saving. In general, workers will be willing to give up in current compensation something less than the amount required to obtain the full amount of the present value of the additional pension benefits.

To the extent that workers will not exchange enhanced pension plan benefits for current compensation, either the employer, confronted with a net increment in the cost of labor services, will have to reduce his work force to that level where its productivity warrants the additional compensation or he will be forced to terminate his plan.

For any given rate of increase in workers' productivity, the effect of these increases in private pension plan costs on the future growth of these plans will depend on (1) covered workers' valuation of the

[66] They may also be willing to substitute the additional saving in the pension plan for other saving in order to maintain substantially unchanged levels of current consumption.

benefits therefrom, in terms of the increase in the risk-adjusted present value of their retirement income and (2) the extent to which they are willing to forgo current compensation or other saving for these additional benefits. If workers value the increase in the worth of pension plan benefits significantly less than the increase in cost to their employers, clearly the future expansion of pension plans will be slowed.

Since the enactment of ERISA, the rate of private pension plan termination has accelerated sharply, far beyond anticipations. To what extent this is attributable to one or more specific provisions of the act (including the substantial increase in paperwork and other compliance costs it entails), or to the coincident sharp business recession, are questions we are not prepared to answer in this study. Nor are we prepared to forecast whether the dramatic surge in terminations will continue, or whether the creation of new plans and the overall growth of the private pension system will be seriously retarded, in response to ERISA's provisions. The impact of the legislation is clearly adverse to pension plan growth; the magnitude of this effect should be the subject of additional investigation.

There are also indications that IRAs are increasing rapidly in number and in amount of assets, although there are as yet insufficient data to quantify this development. Whether this will become a significant trend will depend, in large part, on whether new efficiency gains for pension plans are discovered and implemented.

Inflation. From the late 1960s, the general level of prices has increased at an accelerated rate, although the year-to-year increases have been highly erratic. From rates ranging for the most part between 1 percent and 3.5 percent [67] from 1947 through 1967, the price level has increased at rates ranging from 4.2 percent to 9.4 percent since then.[68] While the future course of the price level is most uncertain, the prospect of a prolonged inflation experience cannot be dismissed out of hand. Its effects on savings in various forms may significantly affect the growth of private pension plans.

During the strong inflationary surge of the 1970s, the personal saving rate rose substantially above the levels experienced in most of the postwar period. In five of the six years from 1970 through 1975, personal saving as a fraction of disposable personal income ranged

[67] Measured as the percent change in the implicit deflators for gross domestic product.

[68] *Annual Report of the Council of Economic Advisers, 1976* (Washington, D.C.: U.S. Government Printing Office, 1976), Table B-3, p. 175.

between 7.4 percent and 8.3 percent. And except for one atypical year, the highest personal saving rate in the previous twenty-three years (1947–1969) was 6.8 percent. The higher personal saving rate during the past six years has challenged the long-held view that inflation favors consumption as opposed to saving uses of current income. Various explanations of this seemingly paradoxical outcome have been advanced.

One theory points to the decrease in real household net wealth resulting from the severity of the inflation following 1968. "If the higher inflation rate (in the 1970s than in the 1960s) produced a decline in real household net wealth, saving rates may have been raised." [69]

Some rough indications of a decrease in household wealth are to be found in the depressed market value of common stocks and a wide range of debt instruments in the last few years. Whether the decline in the value of these assets exceeded the rise in the value of real and other personal property, and consequently whether household net wealth declined or rose, cannot be readily ascertained. Even assuming that changes in the real value of common stocks are in fact indicative of changes in households' real wealth, the data afford only tenuous support for the idea that a decrease in household wealth increases the saving rate. Over the entire postwar period, 1947–1975, changes in this index of real household wealth "explain" virtually none of the changes in the personal saving rate.[70] For five of the last eight years, a period marked by inflation rates substantially above the average of the preceding postwar years, the change in the saving rate has been in the opposite direction from the change in the real value of common stocks, which appears to support the explanation. But in 1974, the year in which the decline in the real value of common stocks was most precipitous, the personal saving rate also fell.

The data do not suggest any direct relationship between the saving rate and inflation. Over the entire postwar period, 1947–1975, changes in the general level of prices explain (statistically) virtually none of the changes in the ratio of gross private saving to gross national product or in the ratio of personal saving to disposable personal income. The regression of the ratio of gross private saving to gross national product on the percentage change in the implicit deflators for gross national product yields an $R^2 = .066$; regressing

[69] Ibid., p. 65.

[70] Regressing the percentage change in the ratio of personal saving to disposable income against the percentage change in the Standard and Poor index of common stock prices deflated by the consumer price index yields an $R^2 = .004$.

the percentage change in this saving rate on the percentage change in the deflator reduces the R^2 to 0. The statistics for personal saving as a fraction of disposable personal income regressed against the same measures are $R^2 = .013$ and $R^2 = .001$. Since personal saving includes saving through pension plans, which displays a strong time trend, a similar regression analysis was undertaken (for the years 1950–1973) with so-called "discretionary" personal saving, that is, personal saving less pension fund saving. The results were slightly better, but show, nevertheless, that changes in the rate of inflation "explain" very little of the change in the rate of saving.[71]

It might be argued, of course, that these regression results would reflect primarily the insensitivity of saving to the very gradual rate of increase in the price level that characterized most of the postwar period and do not adequately weight the recent experience where the inflation rate so markedly accelerated. If the sharply higher inflation rate itself resulted in an increase in the personal saving rate, this should presumably be reflected in changes of the same sign in the saving rate and in the rate of increase in the price level. That is, an increase in the inflation rate should be associated with an increase in the saving rate; a decrease in the percentage increase in the price level should be associated with a decrease in the saving rate. For the eight-year period, 1968–1975, however, the year-over-year change in the personal saving rate was of the same sign as the year-over-year change in either the consumer price index or the GNP deflators in only three years; in the two years (1974 and 1975) in which the increases in either price index were the greatest, the signs of the changes in the saving rate and in the rate of price increase were opposite.

Recent inflation experience appears to have had relatively little effect on the expansion of pension fund saving, which increased by more than 50 percent from 1967 through 1973.[72] To be sure, the largest annual increases in the price level occurred in the years 1974 and 1975 for which the data on pension fund saving are not yet available. It is possible, therefore, that pension fund saving was significantly and adversely affected in those years.

The available data on private pension plan saving also predates the potentially significant interaction of a sharply and erratically rising

---

[71] In the regression of the ratio of "discretionary" personal saving to disposable income on the percentage change in the deflator, $R^2 = .183$ (t value $= 2.2234$); regressing the percentage change in this ratio on the percentage change in the deflator reduces the R^2 to .107 (t value $= 1.5842$).

[72] See Table 7, p. 20.

price level with the provisions of ERISA and of the 1972–1973 social security amendments. For example, if the steep decline in the market value of private pension fund assets in 1974 was directly attributable to the magnitude of the inflation, and had ERISA been applicable in that year, then the inflation would have imposed a substantial increase in employer contributions in order to meet ERISA funding requirements. Future inflation, with the same assumed consequences for the market value of equities and debt instruments, obviously, would increase annual funding requirements for the private pension system. On the analysis of ERISA's effects presented above, a prolonged inflationary period would, in all probability, substantially impede future pension plan growth. Similarly, extension of recent inflationary experience would trigger substantially larger and more rapid increases in social security, hence in the replacement ratio; insofar as private pension benefits are (improperly) tied to some overall replacement ratio, inflationary experience would again impede the future growth of pension plans.

If for no other reason than the complexity of these interactions, any effort at quantitative estimation of the impact of inflation on private pension growth is highly speculative. Our discussion therefore focuses on the operative effects of inflation without attempting to quantify them.

The data on saving and changes in the price level fail to support generalizations that, contrary to older views, strong inflation tends to increase saving uses of current income. Neither, to be sure, do the data imply that inflation per se depresses the rate of saving. Changes and expectations of changes in the price level do enter into decisions about saving-consumption uses of current income, but the view advanced here is that the saving response to inflation is highly variable and cannot be readily generalized. (See Appendix B for a detailed examination of the problems involved in estimating the effects of inflation.)

The saving response depends on how inflation affects real income and the relative costs of consumption and future income. An increasing price level cannot, obviously, erode the real income of all economic entities. The distribution of inflation gains and losses is likely to be widely dispersed and dependent on a large number of factors, including the changes in relative prices throughout the economy. For purposes of this discussion it suffices to think of three groups of income claimants—those obtaining their income from providing labor services, those providing capital services, and government. If government's share of rising nominal income is unchanged by inflation, a decrease in real labor income necessarily means an increase in real capital income. If government's share increases because, for instance, revenues generated by taxes imposed at graduated rates increase more rapidly than nominal income, then either real labor or capital incomes or both may decrease. A decrease in one group's share clearly means that one or another or both of the other shares must increase. These alternative changes in real income are likely to be associated with alternative changes in the relative real costs of saving and consumption.

Consider first the (unlikely) case in which inflation does not alter the real incomes of any of the three claimant groups. This implies that workers expect their nominal compensation to increase at a rate equal to the sum of the rates of productivity and general price level increases, that the nominal returns to capital will increase at a rate equal to the algebraic sum of the rate of change in the productivity of capital and the inflation rate, and that government tax revenues derived from both will increase no more rapidly than the nominal labor and capital incomes.

Such an assumption of constant real incomes may be associated with zero changes in the relative costs of consumption and saving, and in the costs of private sector uses of production inputs relative to governments' costs thereof. These constant overall relative costs do not preclude a wide range of changes in particular relative costs, hence shifts in the composition of production and aggregate demand. While the nominal rate of return on some saving may increase more than proportionately to the expected inflation rate and that on others may rise less, the overall nominal rate of return will rise sufficiently to leave the cost of saving unchanged relative to the cost of consumption. In this case, then, no change in the rate of saving results from the inflation.

Next, consider the case in which inflation results in an equiproportionate decrease in the expected real incomes of both labor and capital services: that is, the inflation involves a real income transfer to government. An equiproportionate decrease in real capital and labor income may be assumed to involve no initial change in the relative costs of consumption and saving. But since the nominal demand for future income decreases more than in the preceding case, while the nominal cost of supplying any amount of future income falls less, saving will decrease.

A third case is that in which the expected inflation is perceived as depressing real labor income relative to real capital income. This case may involve net transfers to or from government but it is most easily illustrated, without affecting the direction of results, on the assumption that government neither gains nor loses on balance. The assumption that expected real labor income will be depressed relative to expected real capital income is likely to be equivalent to assuming that the cost of consumption will increase relative to the cost of future income. The result of the market adjustment in this case would be an increase in saving, hence a reduction in current consumption.

Finally, the inflation may be expected to reduce real capital income relative to real labor income, hence to increase the cost of saving more than the cost of current consumption. This case is likely to be associated with a net transfer to government, with a disproportionate share of the transfer coming from capital income, that is, from the returns to saving.[73] Even if government neither gains nor loses, however, the rise in the general level of prices may entail less of an increase in output prices than in nominal wage rates, hence a reduction in the real returns to saving. The result in this case is a decrease in saving and to a greater extent than in the second case.

On the basis of this analysis, it is not possible confidently to delineate the effects of prospective inflation on saving unless one can confidently specify the relevant characteristics of the inflation. Even more obscure are the inflationary effects on the flow of saving through the private pension system, hence on the growth of private pension plans.

For example, if one ignores the possible inflation-triggered ERISA and social security effects on private pension plans, it does not necessarily follow that an inflation which reduces total saving will similarly affect pension plan saving. Inflation, particularly of the magnitude of recent years, tends to expose workers' wages and salaries to increasingly high marginal income tax rates. By the same token, it tends to increase the efficiency gains afforded by pension plans insofar as these gains are attributable to the tax-sheltering of pension plan saving. Other things being equal, such expansion of these efficiency gains would increase workers' demands for the future income claims afforded by pension plans. Saving through the private pension system, accordingly, would tend to increase as a share of total saving and might very well increase absolutely.

On the other hand, inflation is likely to affect employers' costs of providing pension benefits, even ignoring the ERISA-inflation inter-

[73] Among other reasons, this is likely to be so because inflation disproportionately reduces the real value of capital consumption allowances which are based on historical costs. This leaves an excessive share of the gross returns on capital exposed to income taxes.

action. If the inflation involves an increase in the cost of private pension plan saving, that is, if the percentage increase in the nominal return on pension assets is less than the rate of inflation, employers will face increases in the costs of funding any given amount of real benefits. These are likely to be the circumstances in which employees will be less willing to substitute additional nominal pension fund contributions for current wage and salary payments, because they will want to reduce the saving uses and increase the consumption uses of their current disposable income (as shown above and in Appendix B). On this account, an extended inflation with these characteristics would tend to impede the growth of private pension plans. The incremental efficiency gain from the additional tax sheltering of pension plan saving would tend to offset this impediment, but the net effect is not readily predictable. It is possible, however, that even with an inflation-induced decrease in total saving, the private pension system's growth might not be retarded; indeed, it might well be accelerated.

An inflation in which the relative cost of saving decreases would, on this account alone, reduce employees' costs and at the same time increase employees' demand for retirement income, hence encourage pension plan growth. The additional value of the tax shelter, resulting from the higher marginal tax rates to which employees' wages and salaries would be exposed, would add impetus to private pension expansion.

Taking account of the interaction of ERISA's provisions and inflation, the consequences for private pension plan growth are ambiguous. For example, in each of the alternative inflation cases described above, one of the market outcomes is an increase in the nominal yield on claims to future income. This implies a decrease in the nominal market value of outstanding financial claims with fixed contractual yields (that is, most debt instruments); in some cases, it may also result in a decrease in the nominal market value of equities. On balance, the market value of pension fund portfolios may fall. Under the funding provisions of ERISA, to the extent that this reduction in the value of defined-benefit pension fund portfolios results from decreases in equity values, employers may be required to increase their contributions in order to amortize these losses. In the short run, inflation may result in an increase in the flow of contributions into such pension funds and subsequently into the capital market. But any such expansion of pension plan saving on these terms is likely to be offset in some part over the longer run by retardation in the growth of pension plans in response to the increase in employers' required funding costs. The extent of this offset, clearly, cannot be generalized.

ERISA's fiduciary responsibility provisions may impel untoward changes in portfolio policies under inflationary circumstances or expectations. These provisions permit bonds and other fixed-income securities to be valued at cost so that the decline in their market value under inflationary conditions does not result in experience losses until the bonds are sold. In response both to the funding requirements and to their personal liability, fiduciaries are likely to weight pension fund portfolios more heavily with bonds and other fixed-income securities than they would if guided only by market considerations for maximizing the value of the portfolio over the planning period. Such a portfolio policy is likely to result in a lower overall yield, and the lower the yield, the larger the employers' contributions must be to fund the benefits provided by the plan. As before, the short-term impact of such developments may be an increased flow of employer contributions through pension funds into the capital markets. The corollary thereof, however, is an increase in employers' costs that is likely to slow growth in pension plans over time.

The prospect of prolonged inflation at rates similar to those of recent years may imply a greater displacement of private saving by the expansion of social security than that based on the standard assumption of a 4 percent average annual rate of increase in the consumer price index. Whether displacement would be increased would depend significantly on the inflation's characteristics and on whether the more rapid expansion of social security associated with increased inflation would involve an increase or decrease in workers' permanent income. If workers' permanent income is reduced, the displacement of their demands for private retirement claims is likely to be less severe than if it is increased. This displacement effect might be further modified—indeed it might be more than offset—if the inflation involves a reduction in their real income. Whether rapid inflation and its effects on the growth of social security would reduce or expand the demand for future income thus cannot be generalized. Still less is it possible to generalize the consequences of this interaction for the future of private pension plans.

The main thrust of our entire discussion has been that the growth of private retirement plans depends principally on the efficiency gains such plans afford their participants. ERISA, as we have shown, tends to reduce these gains in employer pension plans of the present configuration and this tendency is accentuated under inflationary conditions. It does not follow, however, that private pension plans have exhausted their capacity for innovations to augment the efficiency gains they provide. Moreover, ERISA's provisions creating individual retirement accounts and liberalizing annual contributions to Keogh plans of the self-employed enhance the potential gains available to individual savers, hence should stimulate retirement saving. The ultimate effects on the flow of saving to private pension plans and other saving arrangements of such factors as ERISA, prospective changes in social security, and the possibility of extended periods of strong and erratic inflation cannot be accurately predicted at this time. However, the history of private pension plans is one of highly diversified adaptation to changing conditions. There is little reason to expect the pension system to lose this adaptability.

APPENDIX A

Analysis of the Effects of Social Security on Private Saving

In his article, "Social Security, Induced Retirement, and Capital Accumulation,"[1] Martin Feldstein presents an extended life-cycle model of consumption and saving behavior. This model is designed to estimate the impact of social security on personal and total saving. His empirical findings suggest that social security has substantially reduced personal saving. The reduction is in part attributed to the effect of payroll taxes in reducing workers' disposable income and in part to the consequence of an increase in consumption resulting from social security's assumed effect in increasing individuals' net wealth. The latter effect was estimated by applying a marginal propensity to consume (currently) social security wealth to the total estimated value of such wealth.

Feldstein's analysis contains a number of conceptual and technical deficiencies which, accordingly, cast doubt on his estimates. One such conceptual error is found in the redundancy of the variables in his consumption function. Adopting the specification of the consumption function used by Ando and Modigliani, Feldstein then adds a retained earnings variable to reflect the impact of corporate saving on household consumption and introduces a social security wealth variable as well. The specification of the function on which his estimates are based is:

$$C_t = a + b_1 Y_t + b_2 RE_t + c_1 W_{t-1} + c_2 SSW_t$$

where, C_t = consumer expenditure,
Y_t = permanent income, a distributed lag on past values of disposable income,
RE_t = corporate retained earnings,

[1] See footnote 18 of the text.

W_t = the stock of household wealth, excluding social security wealth,
SSW_t = estimated social security wealth, and
a, b_1, b_2, c_1, c_2 = coefficients of the variables.

There is obvious redundancy in including (1) a distributed lag disposable income term to represent permanent income and (2) a household wealth term which is, in fact, the capitalized value of that fraction of the permanent income variable which represents saving. Moreover, Feldstein specifies current corporate retained earnings with a positive sign as an argument in the function—that is, consumption outlays are a positive function of current corporate retentions. But corporate retained earnings, if introduced (as they should be) in household accounts, must enter as current saving. Feldstein's formulation thus provides the fascinating assertion that household current consumption is a positive function of household current saving. In addition, there is obvious redundancy in including retained earnings—the capitalized value of a part of household's future capital income streams, hence part of its wealth—and total household wealth as separate variables.

The error most puzzling and most serious in its effect on the quantitative estimates of the impact of social security on private saving is Feldstein's estimation of social security wealth. Of two alternative measures, one gross and one ostensibly net of payroll taxes, he selects gross social security wealth as the correct specification, arguing that payroll taxes have already been accounted for because the income variable used in estimating the consumption function is disposable income. The conceptually correct approach for Feldstein's purposes is to use the net social security wealth variable. Even if this net wealth variable were used, however, Feldstein's estimates would still be questionable. The real difficulty is that he estimates a positive value for both net and gross social security wealth on the basis of the fact that the benefits to be received by those currently in the work force will be funded in (large) part by the prospective payroll taxes of those yet to enter the labor force. While the system does indeed involve such intergenerational transfers, it does not necessarily follow that net social security wealth, as perceived by those currently employed (whose consumption and saving responses are the subject of the inquiry), is positive. The net social security wealth for current workers is merely the difference between the present values of their anticipated benefits, no matter how they are financed, and their payroll taxes. Our calculations suggest that, for most of the period since the beginning of the social security system, net social security wealth has in fact been negative.

In our calculations we estimate the present value of the payroll taxes a male entrant into the labor force may expect to pay from his entrance age—twenty-two years—to the time of his retirement at age sixty-five, and the present value of his retirement benefits and his wife's survivorship benefits for their respective remaining life expectancies. A similar calculation is made for the average covered male worker of the mean age of the covered worker population. Expected payroll taxes are computed on the basis of the schedule of rates and tax bases designated by statute in the calendar year for which the calculation is made; these are adjusted with respect to an expected increase of 5 percent per year in earnings. Similarly, expected benefits are those to be paid pursuant to the benefit formula provided in the law in the calendar year for which the calculation is made. The calculation was made for every fifth year since 1940 for the twenty-two-year-old male and average-aged male worker in each of these years. (Additional details regarding the calculations are available upon request.)

These calculations show that prior to 1955 the average male worker, one who was thirty-four years old, would have assigned a positive value to his net social security wealth. Thereafter, the average male worker who was the average age in the year for which the calculation was made would have attached a negative value to his social security wealth. For the average thirty-four-year-old male worker in 1970, the present value of then-expected payroll taxes plus the taxes he had already paid, exceeded the present value of then-expected benefits by 193 percent. In the case of the average twenty-two-year-old male in 1945, the present value of his expected taxes was greater than that of his expected benefits. Social security wealth was also negative for the average twenty-two-year-old male in each of the succeeding years for which the calculation was made. In 1970, the present value of expected payroll taxes of a male worker who was twenty-two years old that year was 5.6 times the present value of his expected benefits.

While these estimates are based on only two prototypal individuals, they nonetheless suggest that most workers, given the tax rate and benefit schedules in effect in each time period, would have attached a negative value to their participation in the system during most of the postwar years. Estimates to the contrary are usually ex-post measures of the experience of individuals reflecting ad hoc congressional adjustments in tax and benefit schedules and the windfall gains inevitably bestowed on above-average-aged individuals in occupations brought under the system on an ad hoc basis. The latter effect has largely disappeared now that over 90 percent of the labor force is required to participate. In any case, however, to presume that individual workers were able fully to anticipate such changes and hence to incorporate them into their saving/consumption decisions is unrealistic.

The basic deficiency in the Feldstein analysis and other analyses of this type is that current consumption, hence saving as a residual, is specified as a function solely of one or more wealth variables constrained by current disposable income. What is lacking is any functional relationship between saving and its relative cost. While the direction of the effect of social security on private saving is clearly negative, it is not possible to make accurate estimates of the magnitude of this displacement effect unless changes in the relative costs of alternative forms of saving and consumption are taken into account.

An alternative analysis of the effects of social security on private saving is based on the neoclassical theory of capital and investment, which explicitly relates saving and investment to the relative costs of saving and consumption uses of income and consumption and investment uses of productive services.[2]

To begin with, consider workers' demand for—not quantity demanded of—income for retirement that may be obtained in a market for permanent income streams.[3] Retirement income streams and the sources that provide them need not be different in any material respect from any or all other permanent income streams for which there is a market. On the other hand, retirement income streams may be differentiated in such respects that other permanent income streams are not perfect substitutes. In any event, all such permanent income flows for which there is a market, including retirement income, do not exhaust all of the income flow of the economy; they do not include

[2] This analysis borrows heavily from Milton Friedman, *Price Theory, A Provisional Text* (Chicago: Aldine Publishing Company, 1962), chapter 13, pp. 244-263.

[3] The unit of permanent income streams may be thought of as a dollar per year of income in perpetuity. In an efficient market, the rate of interest establishes equivalence between any finite and permanent income streams; that is to say, the capital value, W, of any finite income stream, discounted at rate r, equals the capital value of an income stream of rW in perpetuity. The duration per se of income streams, therefore, does not differentiate among them. In this discussion, income streams are designated as permanent, that is, numbers of dollars per year in perpetuity; it is clear, however, that this is solely for expositional convenience and that the analysis is equally applicable to income streams of differing duration.

the income generated by human capital since such capital cannot be readily exchanged in a market.

The demand function for retirement income, therefore, is specified by the stock of workers' human capital, by their stock of other sources of permanent income insofar as retirement income is not a perfect substitute for these other permanent income streams, and the relative costs of retirement income, other permanent income from real capital, and consumption. To simplify the exposition, it may be assumed to begin with that retirement income streams are perfect substitutes for other permanent income streams. On this assumption, a different demand function for permanent income streams is associated with different amounts of human capital; the larger the amount of human capital, the greater will be the amount of permanent income streams from nonhuman capital that will be demanded at any given price.

The demand function designates for any given amount of income streams the price per dollar of such income streams that workers will pay. In this context, the price is the amount of current consumption forgone to have a dollar of permanent income. It is, therefore, the reciprocal of the rate of interest.[4]

Any point on this demand curve sets off a condition in which workers have no inclination to change the quantity of permanent income or the amount of their sources, given the designated price per unit. This demand curve depicts alternative amounts of sources of permanent income or alternative amounts of such income workers want to hold at alternative prices, not the flow of saving out of current income.

The demand function for permanent income streams will be negatively sloping—that is, the amount of such permanent income workers will want to have will be greater the lower the price per dollar of such permanent income. Since each such demand function is associated with a given amount of human capital and the income generated thereby, each incremental amount of real capital and the permanent income it affords raises the ratio of nonhuman to human wealth or of permanent income streams from nonhuman wealth to those from human wealth. The higher this ratio, the less

[4] Suppose an individual has $100 per year of income in perpetuity, exchangeable in a market for permanent income streams. If the prevailing interest rate were 10 percent, he could exchange the permanent income stream for a capital sum of $1,000 with which he could buy $1,000 of consumption goods and services. The price per unit of his permanent income, hence, is $\frac{1}{.10}$ or $10.

the utility attached to an incremental unit of nonhuman wealth or an additional dollar of the permanent income it affords.

Consider next the supply of permanent income streams, including retirement income. The sources of these permanent incomes are nonhuman capital instruments, which can be produced at some cost. The cost per dollar of permanent income provided by any given amount of these sources is the amount of other output—that is, of consumption goods—which must be forgone by using productive services to produce permanent income streams instead. For any given amount of such capital instruments, this cost per unit is the reciprocal of the marginal product of that quantity of capital. In turn, the marginal product of any given stock of capital depends on the amount of all other productive services and the production function—that is, the technical relationship between the quantities of various types of output and the quantities of the various types of productive services, given the state of the industrial arts and their implementation in production activity.

Given this cost per unit of alternative amounts of permanent income, the quantity of such permanent income streams—or their sources—which it pays to provide is that at which the price per unit equals this cost. The price per unit is the reciprocal of the interest rate.[5]

Since the sources of these permanent income streams do not include all types of capital (they do not include human capital), the supply function is positively sloping. That is, the greater the quantity of such sources the lower is their marginal product, hence the greater is the amount of alternative output forgone—that is, the greater is the cost—per dollar of permanent income. This results from the fact that the given stock of human capital with respect to which any given supply function for nonhuman capital is specified is presumed to be fixed; increases in the stock of the latter, therefore, result in diminishing returns thereto. In this context, a different supply function is associated with each different amount of human capital; the larger the

[5] Suppose the cost per dollar of some given amount of permanent income were, say, $10, but the interest rate were, say, 5 percent. At this rate of interest, the capitalized value of a dollar of permanent income would be $20, and it would pay to use more of the existing productive services to produce permanent income streams and less to produce consumption goods. Similarly, if the cost per dollar of a given quantity of permanent income were $20 but the interest rate were 10 percent, the capitalized value per dollar of permanent income would be $10, and it would pay to produce less permanent income streams and more consumption goods. The amount of permanent income streams which it just pays to provide and maintain, therefore, is that at which the reciprocal of the interest rate just equals the cost per dollar.

amount of the latter, the greater is the marginal product of any given stock of nonhuman capital, hence the lower is the cost of any given stock. Also, the greater the amount of human capital, the larger is the stock of nonhuman capital associated with any given cost per unit thereof. A similar relationship holds for the state of the industrial arts; the more advanced this state is, the greater is the marginal product of any given stock of nonhuman capital, given the amount of all other productive services.

At this point in the discussion, to be consistent with the simplifying assumption used in specifying the demand function, we must assume that the production of retirement income streams is not differentiated from that of other permanent income streams and that all such permanent income streams from nonhuman capital are perfect substitutes.

Defined as above, the supply curve for permanent income streams (or their sources) is the locus of points designating the cost per dollar of permanent income at which producers of these permanent income streams (or their sources) have no incentive to change the quantity of such sources, either by producing less consumption goods and more capital instruments or by the reverse. This supply curve is a schedule of alternative stocks of sources, to be distinguished clearly from a curve which designates short-run investment flows—that is, production of capital instruments.

The demand and supply schedules delineated above may be represented diagrammatically as in Figure 1. The intersection of the demand and supply functions at Q_0 designates a static equilibrium condition; at the price P_0 there is no impetus for workers to alter the stock of permanent income streams (or the stock of sources of such streams) they wish to hold nor for producers to provide either larger or smaller amounts of permanent income, hence to maintain larger or smaller stocks of the sources of these income streams. At this equilibrium point, the price per dollar of permanent income (or of its sources)—the reciprocal of the interest rate—equals the reciprocal of the marginal product of the stocks of capital generating this amount of permanent income.

In a dynamic environment, either the demand or the supply function or (more likely) both will shift through time. Increasing amounts of human capital will tend to increase the importance attached to permanent income streams derived from nonhuman capital, hence increase the price workers will be prepared to pay per dollar for any given amount of these income streams or increase the quantity of such income streams workers will want to have at any

Figure 1
DISPLACEMENT OF PRIVATE SAVING BY SOCIAL SECURITY
Perfect Substitution

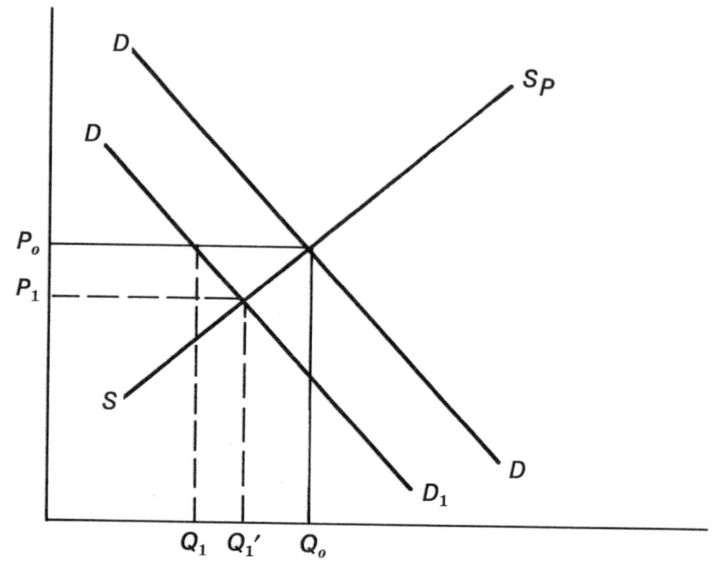

given price. Increases in human capital will also increase the marginal productivity of any given stock of nonhuman capital, hence reduce the cost for any such stock or increase the amount of nonhuman capital which it just pays to maintain at any given cost. A similar effect on the supply function derives from advances in the state of the industrial arts.

These shifts in the demand for and supply of permanent income streams determine changing optimum amounts of such streams or of the stocks of nonhuman capital which generate them. The locus of these equilibrium points traces out the growth path through time of the stocks of these sources. The movement through time from one such equilibrium point to another is, by definition, investment—the use of production capacity to produce the real capital which are the sources of the permanent income streams. By the same token, the adjustment through time from one equilibrium point to another is, by definition, saving—the amount of current income reserved from consumption in order to purchase additional permanent income streams. Since much of the capital which comprises the sources of the permanent income streams is in tangible form, hence exhaustible, the gross amount of saving and investment associated with the movement from one equilibrium point to another on the growth curve exceeds the net addition to the stock of capital which that growth curve depicts.

The equilibrium prices per dollar of permanent income traced out by this growth path are not necessarily constant. Since each such price is determined by the intersection of the shifting demand and supply functions, it will be determined by the magnitude of the shift in the functions and by their respective elasticities. Since any such equilibrium price equals the real rate of interest, the growth path of permanent income from nonhuman capital need not trace out constant real rates of interest.

Within this conceptual context, the social security system may be perceived as presenting workers with an additional "supply" of permanent income. Actually social security annuities cannot be specified as a supply of permanent income as described above. For one thing, there are no producers of such annuities confronting the conditions delineated earlier which determine alternative optimum quantities of such income streams to provide at alternative costs of production. Indeed, the costs of producing alternative amounts of these income streams cannot realistically be specified in the relevant sense of economizing in the use of given amounts of productive services. In fact, a single quantity of this type of income stream at a single "price" is specified by statute, and the specified price does not necessarily represent the opportunity cost of providing the same amount of future income by private producers. There is therefore no schedule of alternative quantities of social security retirement benefits (their capitalized amounts) that will be offered at alternative prices, responsive to the basic economic determinants of private supplies of permanent income streams.

Whether or not workers perceive this distinction between the conditions of supply of privately provided permanent income streams and social security annuities is not pertinent to an analysis of their response to the provision of social security retirement benefits. Any changes in their demands for privately supplied permanent income depends instead on their perception of the substitutability of social security retirement annuities for other privately provided permanent income streams and the relative costs to them of social security and privately provided permanent income.

Suppose, in the first instance, the social security annuities that workers are required to buy are perceived to be perfect substitutes for private annuities; this means, among other things, that the price workers are required to pay for the social security annuities is the same as the prevailing market price they are paying per dollar of privately supplied permanent income. The condition that the price per dollar of social security annuities is the same as that per dollar of privately supplied permanent income means that the discount rate which equates the present value of the expected annuities with the present value of the payroll taxes that workers expect to pay is the same as the prevailing market interest rate—which in an equilibrium condition equals the marginal product of the existing stock of sources of permanent income.

On these assumptions, workers would be indifferent between the amount of social security annuities they are required to have and an equal amount of privately supplied permanent income. Their initial response would be to reduce the amount of the privately supplied permanent income streams they currently own by one dollar for each dollar of the social security annuity stream they are required to have. To be sure, taken by themselves the payroll taxes they are required to pay for the purchase of the social security annuities reduce their aggregate permanent income by reducing the income flow available to them from their providing labor services, including the services of their human capital. But by assumption, this loss is precisely offset by the proceeds from their sale of the nonhuman capital, or its permanent income streams, for which social security annuities are deemed to be a perfect substitute. Initially, upon the substitution of social security for private permanent income, the worker has the same aggregate permanent income and the same rate of consumption as in the equilibrium condition immediately before the introduction of social security.

The dollar for dollar substitution of social security for privately supplied permanent income from nonhuman capital, however, reduces the demand for the latter, as defined above. At any given market price, the worker wishes to have a smaller amount of such permanent income streams, or, equivalently, for any given amount of them, the price he will be willing to pay is less than it was formerly. This may be represented, as in Figure 1, by a leftward shift of the demand for private permanent income streams to DD_1. At their previous market price, the quantity of such income streams demanded decreases from Q_o to Q_1. With the given supply of these permanent income streams, however, their market price cannot remain at P_o. It will instead decline. In the new equilibrium, the price of privately supplied permanent income will be P_1 and the amount of such income streams which will be provided to and held by workers will be Q_1'.

The adjustment to the new equilibrium clearly involves dissaving and disinvestment. The extent of this dissaving and disinvestment is less than it would be if the price of privately supplied permanent income were fixed at its initial level—P_0; it depends, given the magnitude of the shift from DD_0 to DD_1, on the respective elasticities of the demand and supply functions.[6]

In the new equilibrium, the stock of sources of private permanent income streams is less, by $Q_0 - Q_1'$, than it was before the introduction of social security. If government were to use the payroll tax collections to produce perfect substitutes for these privately supplied stocks, total income and wealth would be unchanged. In reality, however, the tax collections are transferred as benefit payments to social security annuitants. Hence, with given amounts of human capital and other productive services, total production capacity and the total flow of income is reduced.

In a dynamic context, the introduction of social security annuities as perfect substitutes for private permanent income streams lowers the growth path of the equilibrium stock of the sources of these income streams. Where these stocks are not fully replaced by government-provided perfect substitutes, the growth path of total income is also lowered. While positive saving and investment continue, the amount of such saving and investment at any point in time is less than it would have been in the absence of social security.

As Figure 1 shows, the price of privately supplied permanent income is lower in the new equilibrium than it was before the introduction of social security. Since this price is the amount of forgone consumption per dollar of permanent income, it is less relative to the price of consumption than it was before social security was introduced. By extension to the dynamic context, the fraction of the reduced flow of disposable income which is saved—that is, used to purchase additional amounts of privately supplied permanent income—will be larger than it was before social security, even though the total amount of such saving will be less.

Now assume that the social security annuities workers are required to purchase are not perfect substitutes for private permanent income streams—that is, the price workers are required to pay for social security annuities exceeds the prevailing market price for private permanent income. In this case, since the price of social security annuities is by assumption greater than that of private permanent income, the substitution of the former for the latter is not as great as in the case of perfect substitution. Moreover, also by assumption,

[6] Moreover, the rate of dissaving and disinvestment—that is, the amount of the reduction per period of time in the stock of private permanent income streams held by workers and afforded by producers—is not determinant in this analysis.

the payroll taxes raise the price of permanent income derived from human capital and from labor services relative to the price of private permanent income from nonhuman capital; workers will, accordingly, wish to have relatively less of the former and more of the latter than in the absence of social security. The demand for private permanent income streams will therefore decrease less than in the case in which social security annuities are a perfect substitute for private permanent income.

This is represented in Figure 2 by the leftward shift of the demand for private permanent income to DD_2. At the previous market price, P_o, the quantity of such income streams demanded decreases from Q_o to Q_2, a smaller decrease than in the first case. With the same supply of these income streams, their market price falls to the new equilibrium level of P_2. At this price, the new equilibrium quantity of private permanent income streams is Q_2', greater than Q_1' in the case of social security annuities which are perfect substitutes for private permanent income.

As in the prior case, the introduction of social security results in dissaving and disinvestment, in the static equilibrium context, and reduces flows of saving and investment through time in the dynamic

Figure 2

DISPLACEMENT OF PRIVATE SAVING BY SOCIAL SECURITY
Cost of Social Security Annuities Exceeds
Cost of Private Retirement Income

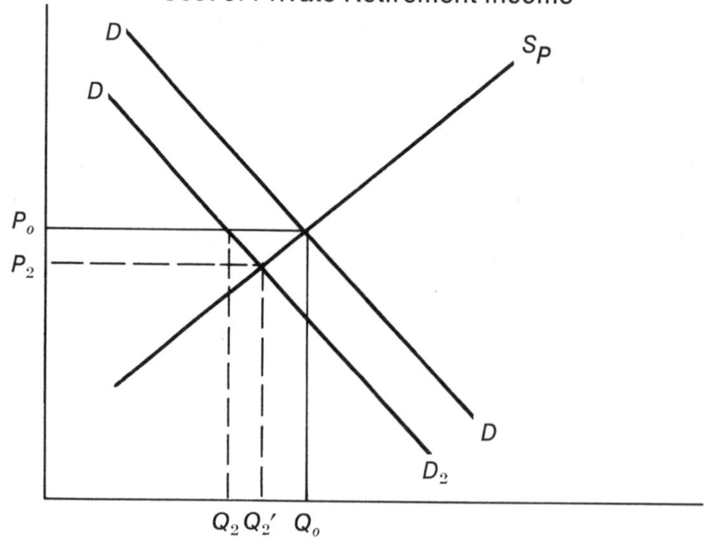

context. But the decrease in the equilibrium stock of sources of private permanent income will be less than in the case of perfect substitutability; in the dynamic context, the reduction in the flows of saving and investment, compared with what these flows are in the absence of social security, will be less than if social security annuities were perfect substitutes. By the same token, the fraction of the reduced flow of disposable income that is saved will be greater than in the absence of social security and greater than in the case where social security annuities are perfect substitutes for private permanent income. Finally, although the amount of total private saving and investment will be less than in the absence of social security, it will be greater than if social security annuities were perfect substitutes for private permanent income, since the decrease in the flow of income will be less than in the first case.

The third case is that in which the "price" of social security annuities is set below the prevailing market price for private permanent income. In this event, the initial effect is a greater inclination by workers to substitute social security annuities for the more expensive private permanent income streams than in the first instance, in which the price of social security annuities is set equal to the prevailing market price of private permanent income. By assumption, moreover, the price of permanent income derived from human capital decreases relative to the price of private permanent income from nonhuman capital. Workers will want to have more of the former and less of the latter than they would in the absence of social security. The demand for private permanent income streams afforded by nonhuman capital will accordingly decrease more than in the first case of social security annuities as perfect substitutes for private permanent income.

In Figure 3, this is represented by the leftward shift of the demand for private permanent income to DD_3. At the market price for private permanent income, P_o, prevailing before social security, the quantity of such income decreases to Q_3, a larger decrease than in the first two cases. With the same supply of private permanent income, their market price falls in the new equilibrium to P_3; at this price, the new equilibrium quantity of private permanent income is Q_3', less than in the preceding cases.

In this case, social security results in greater dissaving and disinvestment in the static equilibrium context and a greater reduction in the flows of saving and investment in the dynamic context than in the prior cases. Similarly, the decrease in the flow of income in the new equilibrium will be greater and both the fraction of that

Figure 3

DISPLACEMENT OF PRIVATE SAVING BY SOCIAL SECURITY

Cost of Social Security Annuities Is Less than Private Retirement Income

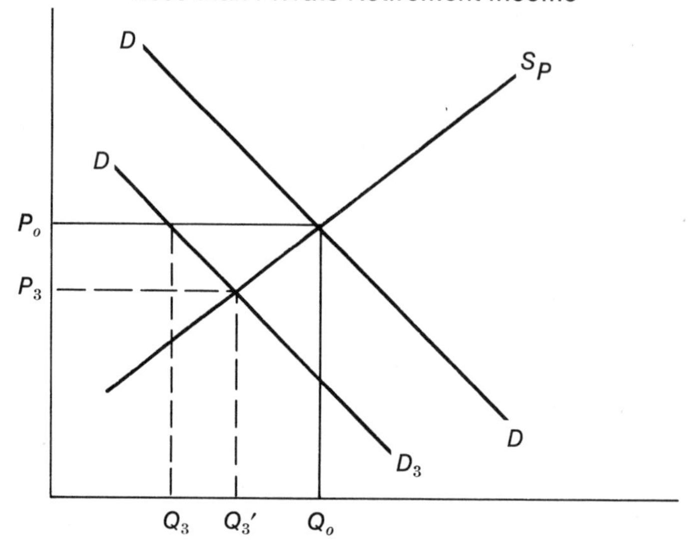

income saved and the amount of saving will be less than in the former cases.

The initial assumption in this analysis was that all permanent income streams from nonhuman capital were perfect substitutes. Relaxing this assumption for the conditions of supply permits analysis of the possible differing effects of social security on the forms or composition of privately supplied permanent income which workers will have. More precisely, the displacement of different private permanent sources—or, in the dynamic context, of different private saving outlets by social security—depends on the respective elasticities of supply of the alternative sources. The more elastic the supply of any such source, the greater the reduction in its stock in the new equilibrium in the static equilibrium context, or the greater the reduction in the flow of saving into additions to the stock in the dynamic context. In any event, except in the unreal case in which the supply of sources is zero-elastic, social security must result in a reduction in the aggregate stock of all private sources, *compared with the stocks that would otherwise be provided.*

A collateral result of this analysis is that expansion of the social security system might result in an increase in workers' provision for retirement through private pension plans *relative to* other private retirement income saving. As noted, the proportionate reduction in the amount of permanent income provided by private pensions and by other private sources (relative to the amount provided in the absence of social security or increases therein) depends on their respective elasticities of supply. In all likelihood, the elasticity of supply of sources provided by pension funds is substantially less than that of other private sources. The amount of these sources provided by pension funds is not subject to frequent variation—the employer cannot freely opt on a year-to-year basis to change the amount of such sources provided as part of a covered employee's compensation; given the plan's benefit formula and the employee's wage, changes in the amount of provision for retirement income require changes in the basic provisions of the plan which will be undertaken infrequently. On the assumption that such institutional "rigidities" are prevalent and substantial, the supply function of retirement income provided by pension plans will be relatively inelastic or at any rate considerably less elastic than that of other private sources. Hence, private provisions for retirement income through pension funds should be expected to increase as a fraction of total private provisions.

On this analysis, the development and rapid growth of the social security system must have reduced private saving and retarded the growth of private provisions for retirement, including private pension plans. The extent of the reduction depends on (1) the "price" of social security annuities relative to that of privately supplied future income, (2) the elasticity of demand for future income, and (3) the elasticity of supply of private future income streams. To repeat, this displacement effect does not preclude increases through time in the amount of private provisions, but it indicates that the rate of any such increase must have been slower than it otherwise would have been.

A rigorous econometric demonstration of the validity of this analysis requires—for each time interval over an extended period—specification and quantification of the functions for the alternative supplies of future income and of the demand for future income and estimation of the present values of social security benefits and taxes. The magnitude of such an econometric effort, however, lies beyond the scope of this study.

APPENDIX B
Effects of Inflation on Saving

Inflation is a highly variable phenomenon. Inflation gains and losses are likely to be widely dispersed and to depend on a large number of factors, including changes in relative prices throughout the economy. However, since an increasing price level cannot erode the real income of all economic entities, it is not possible to generalize the effects of inflation on personal and total private saving.

At a theoretical level, however, it is possible to anticipate the saving response of particular income groups, given expected changes in real incomes and in the relative real costs of saving and consumption. This discussion focuses on three broad groups of income claimants—those obtaining their income from providing labor services, those providing capital services, and government. By making alternative assumptions about the impact of inflation on these groups' relative real incomes, it is possible to delineate the likely changes in the relative costs of consumption and saving, and hence to make observations about the probable change in the amount of current income saved.

The first (unlikely) case assumes that inflation does not alter the real incomes of any of the three claimant groups. This implies (1) that workers expect their nominal compensation to increase at a rate equal to the sum of the rate of increase in their productivity and the rate of increase in the general level of prices, (2) that the nominal returns to capital will increase at a rate equal to the algebraic sum of the rate of change in the productivity of capital and the inflation rate, and (3) that government tax revenues derived from both of these income sources will increase no more rapidly than the rates of increase of these respective nominal incomes.

This assumption of constant real incomes may be associated with a zero change in the relative costs of private consumption and saving and in the relative costs of private and government sector uses of production inputs. This is a reasonable assumption (1) if there is no significant difference between the production functions for consumption and investment goods and (2) if the expected inflation is assumed to involve no change in the composition of demand between consumption and investment outputs. This latter assumption is likely to be consistent with the assumption of an inflation that does not alter the real income of any of the three groups of income claimants.

To be sure, these constant relative costs overall do not preclude a wide range of changes in particular relative costs, and hence shifts in the composition of production and aggregate demand. While the nominal rate of return on some saving may increase more than proportionately to the expected inflation rate and the nominal rate of return on other saving may rise less, the overall nominal rate of return will rise sufficiently to leave the cost of saving unchanged relative to the cost of consumption.

The case is presented diagrammatically in Figure 4. The line *DD* represents the demand for future income with the same arguments

Figure 4

EFFECT OF INFLATION ON SAVING:
No Change in Real Incomes

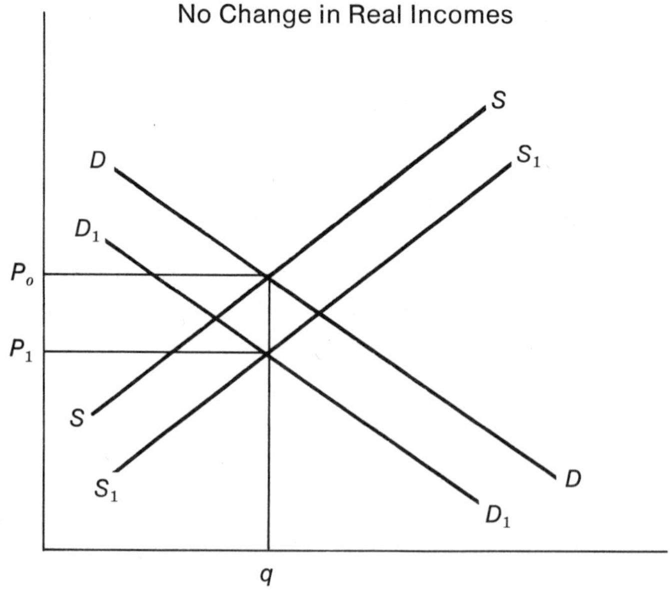

as those delineated in Appendix A. The curve D_1D_1 is drawn to account for the expected increase in the general level of prices, on the assumptions specified for this first case. For any given amount of future income, the nominal cost per dollar must be less than that shown on DD; since this cost is specified as the reciprocal of the rate of return, the difference between DD and D_1D_1 for any given amount of saving is the reciprocal of the anticipated rate of inflation, hence the reciprocal of the required increase in the nominal yield.

The curve SS is the supply of future income in real terms, specified as in the analysis in Appendix A. Under the assumptions of this first case, the curve S_1S_1 represents the nominal supply curve corresponding with SS—that is, the marginal value product, expressed in current rather than constant dollars, of any given amount of capital—which must exceed the real marginal value product by the anticipated percentage increase in the price level. The nominal curves S_1S_1 and D_1D_1 must intersect at the same quantity of future income claims as the corresponding real curves, SS and DD. The difference between P_0 and P_1 is thus the reciprocal of the increase in the nominal yield on the unchanged equilibrium amount of capital, which is equal to the inflation rate.

Next, consider the case in which the inflation results in an equiproportionate decrease in the expected real incomes representing the payments for both labor and capital services—that is, the inflation involves a real income transfer to government. An equiproportionate decrease in real capital and labor income may also be assumed to involve no initial change in the relative costs of consumption and saving.

On this assumption, the demands for consumption and for future income must decrease in equal proportion. The nominal demand for future income—D_2D_2 in Figure 5—must therefore decrease more than in the preceding case. On the same hypothesis, the nominal after-tax return on any given amount of real capital increases less than proportionately to the expected increase in the price level; the nominal cost of supplying any given amount of future income therefore falls less than in the first case—that is, the difference between S_2S_2 and SS is less than that between S_1S_1 and SS. By the same token, the real cost of any given amount of future income must increase—that is, in real terms, the supply of future income becomes $S'S'$. The market adjustment in this case results in a decrease in the optimum amount of future income (hence dissaving) in the static equilibrium context or in a reduced rate of saving in the dynamic context.

Figure 5
EFFECT OF INFLATION ON SAVING:
Equiproportionate Decrease in Real Labor and Capital Income

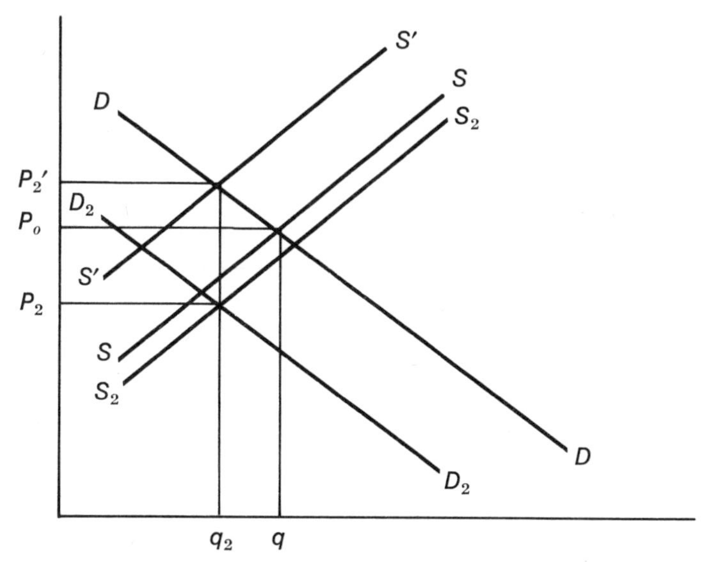

A third case is that in which the expected inflation is perceived as depressing real labor income relative to real capital income. This case may involve net transfers to or from government but it is most easily illustrated (without any difference in the direction of results) on the assumption that government neither gains nor loses on balance. The assumption that expected real labor income is depressed relative to expected real capital income is likely to be equivalent to the assumption that the cost of consumption increases relative to the cost of future income. This equivalence, it is emphasized, does not derive from the notion that labor income is consumed while capital income is saved.

The results of the market adjustment in this case, shown in Figure 6, is an increase in saving, hence a reduction in current consumption. The decrease in the nominal demand for future income—from DD to D_3D_3—is less than in the preceding cases, while the increase in the nominal supply thereof is greater. In this case, the nominal marginal value product of any given amount of capital increases more, hence its nominal cost falls more, in this case than in the preceding cases. In real terms, the supply curve becomes $S'S'$. The equilibrium result, as indicated, is an increase in saving.

Figure 6

EFFECT OF INFLATION ON SAVING:
Decrease in Real Labor Income Relative to Real Capital Income

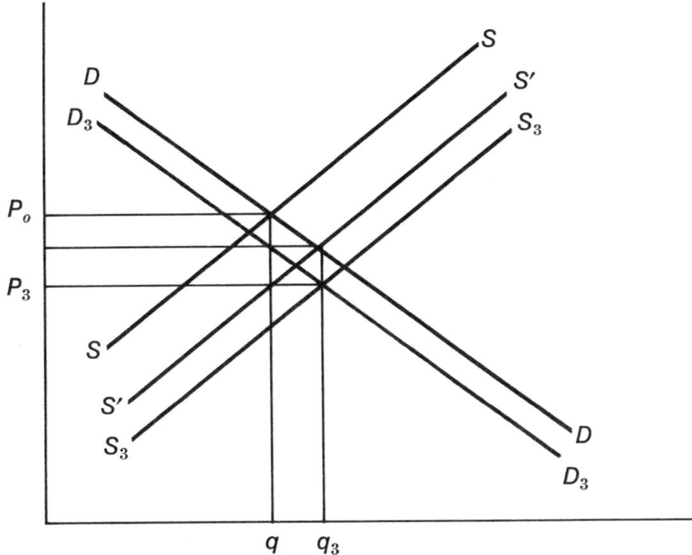

Finally, the inflation may be expected to reduce real capital income relative to real labor income, hence to increase the cost of future income more than the cost of current consumption. This case is likely to be associated with a net transfer to government, with a disproportionate share of the transfer coming from capital income (that is, from the returns to saving). Among other reasons, this is likely to be so because inflation disproportionately reduces the real value of capital consumption allowances based on historical costs. This leaves an excessive share of the gross returns on capital exposed to income taxes. Even if government neither gains nor loses, however, the rise in the general level of prices may entail a smaller increase in output prices than in nominal wage rates and hence a reduction in the real returns to saving.

The results of the market adjustment in this case are, as one would expect, a decrease in the desired amount of future income and in greater proportion than in the second case described above. The demand curve in nominal terms becomes D_4D_4, as shown in Figure 7, and the decrease in the nominal demand for future income exceeds that of the preceding cases. By assumption, the nominal marginal value product of any given amount of capital decreases, and the

Figure 7
EFFECT OF INFLATION ON SAVING:
Decrease in Real Capital Income Relative to Real Labor Income

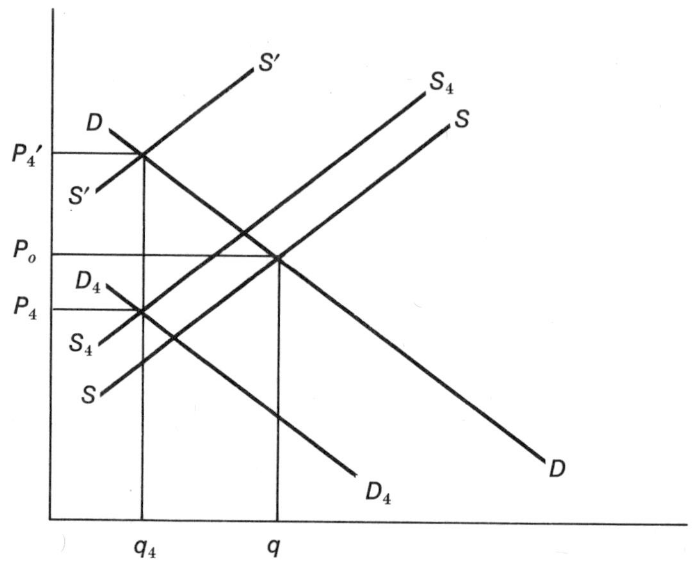

nominal cost of any given amount of capital increases—that is, the nominal supply of future income becomes S_4S_4. In real terms, the supply curve becomes $S'S'$. In the new equilibrium, the nominal yield on capital will have increased less than the increase in the general level of prices and the real return will have fallen. In the static equilibrium case dissaving of $q - q_4$ occurs; in the dynamic context, a substantial reduction in the real rate of saving takes place.

Each of these cases has assumed that the inflation is expected. The contrary assumption may produce different results temporarily until information about the compositional changes in prices as well as changes in average prices is acquired and expectations are revised. But unless the observed rise in prices is deemed to be a "one-shot" phenomenon—that is, unless the revised expectations are that future price changes will conform with the pattern that prevailed before the unexpected increase in the price level—the general results are likely to be akin to one of the alternatives discussed above.

On the basis of this analysis, it is not possible confidently to delineate the effects of prospective inflation on saving unless one can confidently specify the relevant characteristics of the inflation. Even more obscure are the effects on the flow of saving through the private pension system and hence on the growth of private pension plans.